I0111124

Mindfulness

Five Ways to Achieve Real Happiness, True Knowledge and Inner Peace

ABÚ-JALÁL NJ BRIDGEWATER

(FIVE WAYS TO BE, BOOK 1)

ISBN: 978-0-9957369-1-7

Table of Contents

Dedication & Acknowledgements

This book is dedicated to my wife, Grace, and my son, Jalál, without whose love and support, this book could never have been written and published.

Special thanks must also go to my mother, Carolyn, who proofread this book, and to my father, Leslie, for inspiring me to think for myself and express my thoughts through art and writing.

Be Mindful – A Poem

Be mindful, reader, always of thine aim,
To find thyself in inner beauty's heart.
Reflect and ponder on thy goal, life's gain
To free thyself from ego's crafty art.

Be generous, be mindful and be free,
For this is life's great mystery enshrined.
Reflect and ponder on these Ways to Be
And find the Path that destiny's outlined.

Burst forth thy cage that holds thee fast and firm.
A door there is the key to which is hid.
Escape from earthly snares and casket's worm.
Eternal peace, to happiness I bid.
Abú-Jalál thus sets you on this journey true
And shares with you these gems, what a glorious view!

- Abú-Jalál NJ Bridgewater

Preface

Have you ever wondered how to bring balance to your life, or how to attain true happiness and inner peace? Have you wondered if real happiness can ever be obtained? Or is happiness, only the accumulation of material goods?

**"Truth indeed is the sweetest of things;
and that life they call the best which is
lived with understanding."1**
– Gautama Buddha

What does it mean to *be*? How can we live happy and successful lives? How can we live in harmony with ourselves and with others? What is true prosperity? What is the meaning of life? These are questions which have been pondered and discussed throughout the ages. Countless philosophers, thinkers and poets have described the human condition, considered the nature of the world around us and tried to make sense of reality. Some have found hope in the material nature of humanity and our progress as social animals. Others have sought to speculate on the metaphysical nature of reality. Yet others have come up with practical steps and teachings which can help us to live—to *truly* live—as we are supposed to: to live a life of fulfilment, harmony, inner peace and satisfaction. True happiness, true wealth and prosperity, does not consist in material things. This is a great truth that we must all acknowledge before we set out on the path of self-realization and spiritual transformation.

I have often wondered about these questions and one of my life's goals has been to try to uncover answers, as well as practical steps, which can lead to true happiness and fulfilment. I have read various key works of philosophy, religion, history and self-development and have tried my best to discover the gems and pearls hidden within each. In the course of writing this book, I have delved into a number of works which each contain a wealth of information on spirituality, meaningful living and inner happiness. These can be found in the bibliography at the end of this book. I have chosen poignant quotations from each key work which will help us to focus our minds on important truths of self-realization. You will find these scattered throughout the various chapters.

These quotations will serve as useful focal points for meditation and contemplation and I would recommend that you revisit them from time to time in order to refresh your memory of the points we have covered. I hope that you will find them inspirational and motivating. I have marked these key quotations in bold. Other quotations throughout the book are used to illustrate various points of interest.

This is a short book—but it is also a potent one. True wisdom is not complicated. It is found in the simplicity of contemplation, in the beauty of nature and the stillness of silence. It is not something which requires advanced degrees or an exhaustive study of philosophy. True wisdom is to know what is most important in life, to understand who we are and how we are supposed to live our lives. Very often, the truly wise are actually the *least* educated. Sometimes a sifter of wheat or a baker is aware of greater and more potent truths than the most erudite scholar or the most well-respected academic. This is because acquired learning often gets in the way of *real* understanding. And real understanding is simplicity itself. It is not found in the noise and confusion of technology and hustle and bustle of urban living.

Rather, it is found in the light which burns within each one of us. It is found in the essential nobility and spirituality of each human being and how that behoves us to be. As Gautama Buddha said: **"Well-makers lead the water (wherever they like); fletchers bend the arrow; carpenters bend a log of wood; wise people fashion themselves."**[2] The development of this kernel of wisdom and understanding is the goal of this book.

As the title of this book suggests, I have focused on Five Ways to Achieve Real Happiness and Inner Peace. What I mean here by 'ways' is paths, or steps, which are, in reality, all parts of one path. They all lead to one goal but we must tread through each one of these paths before we can reach a state of true balance, which I call **equanimity**. In Buddhism, this is called the Middle Path, and in Islam is referred to as the Straight Path. The Greek philosopher, Plato, refers to this path as the "heavenly way". In *The Republic*, he writes: **"Wherefore my counsel is, that we hold fast ever to the heavenly way and follow after justice and virtue always, considering that the soul is immortal and able to endure every sort of good and every sort of evil."**[3] This, it could be said, is the essence of equanimity. It involves treading a middle path between extremes and maintaining a standard of justice and virtue in all aspects of our lives. The great Chinese mystic, Laozi, refers to this path as 'The Way' (*Tao*), which is the central focus of the *Tao Te Ching* (also spelled *Daodejing*). I have gleaned words of wisdom from all of these works.

The Five Ways to Be described in this book are as follows: (1) Detachment and Virtue, (2) Radiant Acquiescence, (3) Magnanimity, (4) Contemplation, and (5) Enkindlement. All of these are steps to achieving a state of **mindfulness**, true equanimity, contentment, happiness, joy, and true wealth and prosperity. These five paths, or steps, are the essence and core of the highest philosophies and codes of wisdom throughout all ages of history. Simply reading those five phrases, however, is not sufficient to achieve or realise them in our lives. Rather, they should be understood as markers, or tokens, for much deeper spiritual concepts which only time and spiritual receptivity will allow us to fully uncover. Nevertheless, as noble, spiritual beings, we are all capable of getting to grips with these realities and walking this path of enlightenment. Indeed, the goal of every religion or philosophy is to realise and achieve the essence of these principles. The core of each one can be found scattered throughout numerous texts, often couched in terminology that requires familiarity with a particular religious tradition or school of thought. This book will aim to decode this ancient wisdom, which I call the **philosophy of equanimity**, and allow everyone to benefit therefrom.

> **"There are three things extremely hard: steel, a diamond, and to know one's self."**[4]
> - Benjamin Franklin

I have divided this book into fifteen chapters and a bibliography. Every three chapters will deal with one of the Five Ways to Be. In the first, the concept will be introduced through a parable, which is a powerful tool to distil and elucidate divine wisdom. In the second of each set of chapters, we will introduce a **practice** which will assist you in releasing the power of each Way. Finally, in the third chapter, we will introduce some **steps for further development**. These will help us to bring our ideas into practice, so that we can develop greater spiritual practice as well as understanding. Understanding, on its own, is good, but it is not enough for living a truly fulfilling and meaningful life. Rather, only by living these Ways of Being as our way of life can we achieve true fulfilment. As the sage, Laozi, has said: **"He who knows other men is discerning; he who knows himself is intelligent. He who overcomes others is strong; he who overcomes himself is mighty. He who is satisfied with his lot is rich; he who goes on acting with energy has a (firm) will."**[5] Some questions for reflection at the end of each chapter will help you to focus on the main ideas and may be useful points of discussion when the book is read in a book club or study group.

This book is a message for a troubled world, and it is important that you share it as widely as possible. As more people learn how to live in equanimity and mindfulness, we will gradually be able to overcome the hate, violence and discord which so plagues the world we now live in. Inner harmony, peace and prosperity are, ultimately, the necessary prerequisite to world harmony, peace and prosperity. Confucius said: **"Let the superior man never fail**

reverentially to order his own conduct, and let him be respectful to others and observant of propriety:—then all within the four seas will be his brothers. What has the superior man to do with being distressed because he has no brothers?"[6] As long as we live discordant lives, we will never be able to live in harmony with one another. That is why I hope that this book will have the widest impact possible. Please make sure to share it with your friends, on blogs, Twitter, Facebook, and other mediums. Also, please make sure to leave a review on Amazon.com or Amazon.co.uk so that this book can be as widely shared as possible.

If you find this book helpful, in any way at all, or even if you find it wanting in some capacity, your Amazon and blog reviews will be appreciated. For further updates on other books as they are released, please make sure to follow me on Twitter @Nicholas19 and @equanimityblog

When not involved in writing, teaching and travelling, I am engaged in promoting and supporting *Msingi wa Tumaini* (Swahili for 'Foundation of Hope'), a charitable organization which I co-founded with my wife, Grace Bridgewater, in 2012. For more information, please follow Msingi wa Tumaini on Twitter @mwtumaini, like Msingi wa Tumaini on Facebook, and/or visit mwtumaini.org. Please bear in mind that Msingi wa Tumaini has no affiliation with the *Five Ways to Be* series and is an organization solely dedicated to helping orphans and vulnerable children in Kenya, particularly in the village of Uyoma on the coast of Lake Victoria in Western Kenya, near the city of Kisumu. Your donations and support for Msingi wa Tumaini will be greatly appreciated and will help to change lives, enabling girls and other vulnerable children to gain access education, as well as supporting child protection training and other charitable activities. Helping others is an essential element of true mindfulness and equanimity.

> **"Withhold not good from them to whom it is due, when it is in the power of thine hand to do it. Say not unto thy neighbour, Go, and come again, and to morrow I will give; when thou hast it by thee... He that despiseth his neighbour sinneth: but he that hath mercy on the poor, happy is he."**[7]
>
> – The Book of Proverbs 3:27-28, 14:21

It would be appropriate here to reflect on the words of Confucius, that Master of Wisdom, who was asked what constitutes the superior man. He replied: **"The cultivation of himself in reverential carefulness."** When asked by his disciple, **"And is this all?"**, he replied: **"He cultivates himself so as to give rest to all the people."**[8] I hope that this book, *Five Ways to Achieve Real Happiness, True Knowledge, and Inner Peace*, may serve as one more contribution to giving 'rest to all the people'. The path to self-realization is not easy, but is worthwhile, and I encourage you to set out on this path with earnestness and determination. Nothing worthwhile is without difficulty, and often the most difficult obstacles are the ones which give us the greatest learning and development. This requires focus, and it requires dedication on the part of each one of us. In this vein did Confucius say: **"The man of virtue makes the difficulty to be overcome his first business, and success only a subsequent consideration;—this may be called perfect virtue."**[9] May we all strive to achieve perfect virtue!

Thanks again for downloading this book, I hope you enjoy it!

- Abú-Jalál NJ Bridgewater

(January 2017)

I. FIRST WAY TO BE – DETACHMENT & VIRTUE

Parable – Diogenes of Sinope

There once was an eccentric philosopher by the name of Diogenes (b. 419 BCE), who was a native of the city of Sinope. He was well-known for his plainness of living and of dress.[10] He had few possessions, including a bag, and he did not even have a staff until he started to grow infirm. Afterwards, he would carry it with him wherever he went. All in all, his possessions consisted of the bag, his staff, a bowl for drinking water and the cloak on his back. He had no house or home and would sleep wherever he was able, folding his cloak so that he could sleep in it. He even had no shoes, as he would walk upon the snow barefoot. Then, one day, he observed a child who was drinking water with his hands and realised that his bowl was an extravagance. He remarked: "A child has beaten me in plainness of living", at which point he threw away his bowl.[11]

Reflections:

The first of the Five Ways to Be is detachment and virtue. What does this story tell us about detachment? Diogenes of Sinope was an ascetic who had abandoned every physical pleasure and attachment. Rather than taking this story literally, however, let us try to look at it from the perspective of symbolic meaning. A parable is a simple story which is used to represent or teach a moral or spiritual lessons. Powerful examples of these can be found in the Gospels of Jesus Christ, as well as in the Qur'ān, Sufi literature and Buddhist writings.

Now, let us try to decode this story and find out what the moral lesson is. Diogenes represents each one of us, and we all have numerous material, emotional and even ideological attachments which usually form the basis of our everyday lives. We do not just work to live and satisfy our basic needs. In most cases, we are also working to enjoy material pleasures and to satisfy our desire for entertainment. Likewise, we have emotional attachments to family, friends, partners, or even pets, places and things. We also have ideological attachments to our beliefs, prejudices, dogmas and conceptions.

All of these attachments tie us down and prevent us from developing our true inner selves. They are like baggage which weigh us down and prevent us from making progress. Diogenes believed that he was detached from all of these things. He took things to the extreme, being an ascetic who wandered from place to place and did not own a house or even shoes. Nevertheless, he came to realise that he was not truly detached because the bowl that he possessed was yet another unnecessary and frivolous item which was not truly necessary.

So what can we learn from this story? The bowl represents Diogenes' attachment to the material world and all that is therein. Let us imagine that the bowl is the totality of all of his attachments, including emotional ties and ideological baggage. When he realised that these things were preventing him from attaining true detachment and happiness, he smashed the bowl and embraced true freedom. Real freedom is to be detached from the material and aware of spiritual reality. Attachment to the material world is a barrier between the soul—the inner being of each human—and the vast and limitless potentialities of the spiritual world.

"Let a man leave anger, let him forsake pride, let him overcome all bondage! No sufferings befall the man who is not attached to name and form, and who calls nothing his own."

- Gautama Buddha, *The Dhammapada*, Ch. XVII., v. 221[12]

We can imagine that we are all like birds trapped within a cage. Imagine also that the door of the cage is closed, but not locked. Most of us are unaware that there is a door, and even those that are aware of the door, think that it is locked. All that is required to escape from the cage is to push open the door and leave behind the cage and all that is contained therein. The cage represents all our attachments—material, emotional and ideological. Most of us are unwilling to consider even leaving the cage, because we believe it is all that is. What if, however, there is a whole world beyond the cage, even more magnificent and beautiful, full of limitless energy and boundless joy? What if we can escape from the cage of attachment and embrace a higher reality?

We can escape this cage. We can break the bowl of attachment. But how? Unlike Diogenes, we do not actually need to practise asceticism, which represents an extreme. Remember, we are trying to practise the Middle Path—the Middle Way—so both the extremes of material overindulgence and asceticism are to be avoided. We do not want to literally follow the path of Diogenes of Sinope. However, what we do want to do is release ourselves from the chains and cage of attachment and embrace the boundless energy of the spirit. The way to do this is through the development of **virtue**, the other key element of the **First Way to Be**. We should lead a life that is both virtuous and detached.

> **"The Master said, Is virtue a thing remote? I wish to be virtuous, and lo! virtue is at hand.'"**
> - Confucius, *Confucian Analects*, Book VII, Chapter XXIX.[13]

Virtue, as a singular noun, means behaviour which follows a high moral standard. This means, essentially, being a good person and having an exemplary character. To become virtuous, we must develop individual virtues. These include, for example, love, kindness, tolerance, generosity, politeness, cleanliness, dignity, honesty, trustworthiness, integrity, uprightness, patience, forbearance, respectfulness, chastity, pureness of thoughts, perseverance, steadfastness, fortitude, and so on. There are too many individual virtues to enumerate them all here. However, do not be disheartened by this list, as no-one can attain perfection and no-one can acquire all of these virtues in one day, or even in a lifetime. We can only develop them one by one and try to improve our characters on a daily basis. We will look at some ways that we can do this later on.

The Story of the Three Woes

At this stage, let us now consider another story, which will help us to understand how to develop detachment and virtue. It will also give us a good perspective on the nature of suffering and the impermanence of material things. Most people are aware of the story of Siddhartha Gautama, known as the Buddha, but let us repeat it here for illustration. There once was a king by the name of Suddodhana, who had a wife called Māyā-devī. Legend has it that she gave birth at Lumbinī, where there was a beautiful grove of trees. When the child was born, a seer approached the king and said, "Banish all anxiety and doubt. The spiritual omens manifested indicate that the child now born will bring deliverance to the whole world."[14]

When the young prince, called Siddhartha, had grown up, his father wanted him to get married. The prince, however, was not very interested in material things. He loved to sit under a tree in his father's garden and practise meditation. Eventually, Siddhartha chose his cousin, princess Yasodharā, to be his wife. They had a son together called Rāhula. Nevertheless, he maintained a religious attitude to life and regularly bathed in the most holy river of India, called the Ganges.[15]

Now, Siddhartha's father, the king, wanted him to live the happiest life possible, so he made sure that his son did not see any suffering, poverty or death. All sorrowful sights, misery and knowledge of misery were kept away from him so that he would not know that evil existed. However, Siddhartha was eager to see his father's kingdom, so he asked his father for permission to see the city. His father gave him a jewel-fronted chariot with four horses, and all the roads through which he passed were decorated with curtains and banners. As he passed out of the city and into the countryside, he came upon an old man with a bent frame, a wrinkled face and a sorrowful brow. When the prince asked why the man appeared the way he did, the charioteer replied: "These are the symptoms of old age. This same man was once a suckling child, and as a youth full of sportive life; but now, as years have passed away, his beauty is gone and the strength of his life is wasted." Siddhartha was greatly affected by this.[16]

Next, they came upon a sick man by the road, who was gasping for breath, while his body was convulsing as he groaned with pain. The prince asked what kind of man this was. The charioteer replied: "This man is sick. The four elements of his body are confused and out of order. We are all subject to such conditions: the poor and the rich, the ignorant and the wise, all creatures that have bodies, are liable to the same calamity." This affected him yet more.[17]

The charioteer sped up to avoid further such sights. This proved to be impossible, however, as four people passed by, carrying a corpse, and he asked what this was. The charioteer replied again: "This is a dead man: his body is stark; his life is gone; his thoughts are still; his family and the friends who loved him now carry the corpse to the grave." The prince further enquired: "Is this the only dead man, or does the world contain other instances?" The charioteer reluctantly replied: "All over the world it is the same. He who begins life must end it. There is no escape from death." Greatly moved by this sad news, the prince exclaimed: "O worldly men! How fatal is your delusion! Inevitably your body will crumble to dust, yet carelessly, unheedingly, ye live on." Turning around, they returned to the city.[18]

When Siddhartha returned to his wife, she asked him to tell her the cause of his grief. He said: "I see everywhere the impression of change; therefore, my heart is heavy. Men grow old, sicken, and die. That is enough to take away the zest of life." It was then that the young prince resolved to abandon everything and seek out *nirvāna*, i.e. enlightenment. Abandoning his wife and family, and travelling across the land, he practised numerous austerities and deprived himself of food and comfort. This, however, did not allow him to succeed in his goal. Finally, he directed his steps towards a Bodhi-tree and sat beneath its shade. While seated there, he was tempted by the forces of evil, called Māra, who is described as the lord of the five senses and the enemy of truth. When he had conquered Māra, he began to meditate seriously, pondering all the miseries and evils of the world. He then came to the realisation that: "The world is full of evil and sorrow, because it is full of lust. Men go astray because they think that delusion is better than truth. Rather than truth they follow error, which is pleasant to look at in the beginning but in the end causes anxiety, tribulation, and misery." He furthermore recognised that "ignorance was the root of all evil." It was also then that he came to realise the four noble truths, which are: (1) the existence of sorrow, (2) the cause of suffering, (3) the cessation of sorrow, (4) and the eightfold path which leads to overcoming sorrow. It was only by overcoming self that one could achieve true self-realization and happiness.[19]

Happiness and the Material World

What can we understand from this story? Life, in its essence, is passing—fleeting. It is not something which endures. We are all born, we live, and we die. For many, life is all that there is. But there are also millions of others who realise that life on earth is but a small part of existence. Man, in his essence, is a noble being—a soul which endures forever. Death is merely the separation of the relationship between the body and the soul. In *The Republic*, one of his most famous dialogues, Plato says: "But the soul which cannot be destroyed by an evil, whether inherent or external, must exist for ever, and if existing for ever, must be immortal."[20] This is due to the fact that the soul, being something entirely spiritual, exists above and beyond the material world. In the material world, everything is composite, i.e. made of different elements, whereas the soul is a being which is made of one single, spiritual substance. Plato says: "The soul, I said, being, as is now proven, immortal, must be the fairest of compositions and cannot be compounded of many elements."[21] As such, the world and all that is around us, which is material, is something which we should be detached from.

"The Worldly Hope men set their Hearts upon
Turns Ashes—or it prospers; and anon,
  Like Snow upon the Desert's dusty Face
  Lighting a little Hour or two—is gone."

- Omar Khayyam, *The Rubaiyat*, XII.[22]

If we set our hopes upon this world and seek to
achieve the utmost pleasure in this life, we will always
be disappointed and unhappy. In reality, as
Siddhartha realised, the world is full of misery and
pain, death and destruction. Everything passes away,
both wealth and good-fortune, as well as health,
youth, and beauty. Kings pass away and lose their
thrones. In the case of many of them, not even their
names survive. Many queens are not mentioned in
history at all, and few princes receive even the
smallest mention. How many ancient kings had a
hundred sons or more! All of these enjoyed the
greatest pleasure and excess of enjoyment on earth,
yet how many of these do we even know the names of?
Their dead bodies have turned to dust and their
knuckle-bones are indistinguishable from those of
people who lived in the utmost poverty and suffering.
Everything material passes away, so there is no point
in setting our affections on the things of this world.

Marcus Aurelius, the Roman Emperor who was also a philosopher, remarked: "How quickly all things disappear, in the universe the bodies themselves, but in time the remembrance of them."[23]

What, then, is the solution? The way to overcome suffering and find true happiness is to practise virtue. In the *Dhammapada*, Buddha says: "The virtuous man is happy in this world, and he is happy in the next; he is happy in both. He is happy when he thinks of the good he has done; he is still more happy when going on the good path."[24] Likewise, he says: "If a man does what is good, let him do it again; let him delight in it: happiness is the outcome of good."[25] In the Qur'ān also, we find the promise: "Contend earnestly on his path, that you may attain to happiness."[26] So, how can we do that? How can we strive earnestly on the path to happiness? Thankfully, the great teachers of the past have laid out a path for us, which leads not only to happiness—true happiness—but also complete fulfilment and freedom from fear and sorrow. It is a spiritual medicine which leads us to unlock the hidden potential within us and to achieve inner peace and tranquillity.

"Thou canst pass thy life in an equable flow of happiness, if thou canst go by the right way, and think and act in the right way."
– Marcus Aurelius, *Meditations*, Book V.[27]

In the next chapter, we will look at the practices which will lead us to achieve the First Way to Be—how to be detached and virtuous. Many books could, in reality, be written on this topic alone. However, we will give a simplified explanation which will allow anyone to achieve a happy, mindful, detached and virtuous life. Full achievement and realization of virtue is not possible, as we are all imperfect beings. Nevertheless, we all possess an inner nobility that contains limitless potential and power, so we should really see it as an eternal path to perfection, in which we can achieve greater and greater joy and happiness. Each step brings us closer to an everlasting goal.

Questions for Reflection

The following are some questions that will help us to reflect on what we have learned so far:

1. What is the First Way to Be?

2. What is detachment?

3. What is virtue?

4. What is the real nature of man?

5. How can we achieve happiness?

∞∞∞∞∞∞∞∞∞∞∞∞∞∞∞∞∞∞∞∞∞∞∞∞

II. FIRST PRACTICE – THE PATH OF VIRTUE

The first thing you must realize is that you are not simply a body. You are a noble human being filled with hidden treasures and gems that are waiting to be unlocked. You are possessed of infinite and unlimited potential, inner power and strength, and a sea of boundless mystery. As a truly noble and magnificent being, you are capable of achieving your highest potential. As a soul or spirit, you are an eternal being which will transcend death and live throughout all the everlasting depths of time. There is no end to your being, nor is there any end to your journey towards perfection. The purpose of your life is to know the Inner Reality which lies within you and the Higher Being which has brought you into existence. Your purpose is not to become attached to the physical things of this world, which will all die and perish. Your body will inevitably die, your house will inevitably crumble to dust, and all your wealth will be spent, lost or taken by others. So nothing remains of any lasting value but your eternal soul and how to cultivate that soul. Like a garden in need of careful cultivation, so likewise your soul needs to be cultivated with virtue and detachment.

"This is the way, there is no other that leads to the purifying of intelligence. Go on this way! Everything else is the deceit of Mâra (the tempter)."[28]
- Buddha, *The Dhammapada*, Ch. XX, v. 274

We are no masters of this path. We are all simply seekers travelling along the way. Thankfully, however, we are not alone on this journey, because the Creator of the universe has brought into being many Teachers who have given us guidance throughout the ages. One of these is Gautama Buddha, another is Krishna, yet another is Jesus Christ, and so on. The list is endless, as time has neither beginning nor end and there is no limit to God's creation. As there are billions and trillions of stars in the sky, and billions of galaxies which contain them, so likewise are there limitless worlds where intelligent beings like us gaze up at the span and breadth of eternity and wonder why they exist and what their purpose in life is. So the list of Great Teachers, of Inspired Beings who manifest the Will of that Creative Force which brought everything into existence is endless and unlimited. Therefore, it is to their teachings that, ultimately, we must turn when looking for guidance. Likewise, there are numerous philosophers, thinkers and poets who are also inspired, to a lesser and more imperfect degree, by the Creative Force, and these teachers also provide useful guidance and gems of wisdom.

In the last chapter, we read the story of Siddhartha Gautama, afterwards known as Buddha, and his realization of the nature of suffering. His teachings centre on the Eightfold Path, which is an extension of the Four Noble Truths. To recap, the Four Noble Truths are:

- The existence of sorrow
- The cause of suffering
- The cessation of sorrow
- The eightfold path that leads to the cessation of sorrow

The existence of sorrow simply means awareness of the existence of sorrow and the impermanence of all things. As we learned in the previous chapter, Buddha identified the cause of suffering as attachment to the material world. He said: "The world is full of evil and sorrow, because it is full of lust. Men go astray because they think that delusion is better than truth. Rather than truth they follow error, which is pleasant to look at in the beginning but in the end causes anxiety, tribulation, and misery."[29] Furthermore, he explained: "It is sensuality, desire, selfishness; all these things, O brethren, are the origin of suffering. And what is the annihilation of suffering? The radical and total annihilation of this thirst and the abandonment, the liberation, the deliverance from passion, that, O brethren, is the annihilation of suffering. And what, O brethren, is the path that leads to the annihilation of suffering? It is the holy eightfold path that leads to the annihilation of suffering, which consists of, right views, right decision, right speech, right action, right living, right struggling, right thoughts, and right meditation."[30] This is the core and the kernel of the message of the Buddha.

Let us go through the elements of the Eightfold Path one-by-one and find out how we can practice each one.

1. Right view(s) (or understanding)

"Wisdom is the principal thing; therefore get wisdom: and with all thy getting get understanding."[31]
Proverbs 4:7

The various elements of the Eightfold Path are not steps to be followed one-by-one, in sequence. Rather, they are all essential components of a whole. If one element is missing, the whole is incomplete and true liberation from unhappiness and suffering is impossible. Only by following each element of the Eightfold Path laid out by the Buddha can we truly attain to happiness. It is also important to remember that the Eightfold Path is not something unique to Buddhism, and this book does not seek to advocate one particular religion or sect. Rather, the core teachings of the Buddha, which are collectively called the Dharma, are identical to the core teachings of Krishna, Jesus Christ and other teachings, as they are all Teachers of the same Path—which is called the Straight Path. There is no essential difference between any one of these Teachers or their core teachings.

Now, let us try to understand what 'right view' or 'right views' means.

'Right' means correct, true and on the path of guidance. View or views here means understanding. When we build a house, we start, first of all, with the foundations. We do not go straight ahead and build the roof. Rather, we must first dig deep into the ground, and then lay concrete in order to create a solid foundation. If the foundation of the building is solid, the building will be solid. If the foundation is earthquake-resistant, the building will be earthquake-resistant. If the foundations are shaky, the building will not last long. Anything built on the foundation of Truth will last forever and have no end. Ceaselessly, it will continue throughout all time. Anything, however, which is built on the foundation of falsehood, which is the negation of good, is bound to collapse and be utterly obliterated. Nothing endures in this world, neither sovereignty nor wealth, nor even fame or renown. What does endure is good teaching, good principles and wisdom. There is a reason why we do not remember all the aristocrats of ancient Judea, but we remember a carpenter named Jesus of Nazareth, the Son of Mary, because his teachings were founded on Truth.

> **"Therefore whosoever heareth these sayings of mine, and doeth them, I will liken him unto a wise man, which built his house upon a rock: And the rain descended, and the floods came, and the winds blew, and beat upon that house; and it fell not: for it was founded upon a rock.**
>
> **"And every one that heareth these sayings of mine, and doeth them not, shall be likened unto a foolish man, which built his house upon the sand: And the rain descended, and the floods came, and the winds blew, and beat upon that house; and it fell: and great was the fall of it."[32]**
>
> - Jesus Christ, Matthew 7:24 – 27.

So what is this foundation of Truth which we must build our understanding upon? What is this ancient and eternal wisdom which should be the foundation of our lives? In the Bhagavad-Gita, Krishna explains: "Humbleness, truthfulness, and harmlessness, patience and honour, reverence for the wise; purity, constancy, control of self, contempt of sense-delights, self-sacrifice... detachment, lightly holding unto home, children, and wife, and all that bindeth men; an ever-tranquil heart in fortunes good and fortunes evil, with a will set firm to worship Me—Me only! ceasing not... So to attain,–this is true Wisdom, Prince!"

Here, Krishna first lists a number of virtues and practices which will engender happiness and eternal bliss. The practice of virtue is called **piety**. Secondly, he mentions **detachment** and realization of the ephemeral nature of material and emotional ties. Third, he mentions tranquillity in the face of adversity, as well as in times of prosperity. This is what we shall refer to throughout this book as **equanimity**. And last of all, he mentions the need to worship the Higher Power which was manifested through Him—the Creative Force which is the source of all light and power. This we may refer to as **devotion**. These four elements: piety, detachment, equanimity and devotion, are the essential bedrock of wisdom and understanding. Being aware of the nature of suffering and the impermanence of existence, we have developed right view or right understanding.

2. Right decision (thought, or aspirations)

The second element is right decision, thought or aspirations. This may also be referred to as right intention or intentions. This refers to the purposive or intentional thought which appears in our minds. Right understanding means having a correct understanding of the nature of reality, of the nature of suffering and the need for piety, detachment, equanimity and devotion. Right thought means purity of thought, of not intending evil for oneself or others, of having a pure and clean mind and washing away corrupt thoughts and inclinations. Everything is founded on intention, as intention is the basis of action. With the exception of purely involuntary actions, such as reflexes and hiccoughs, our intentions serve as the springboard for all our actions. If we intend evil, how can anything other than evil result? If we think badly of others, how can we be sincere? If we do good with the intention of eventually exploiting others, how can we claim to be righteous? Therefore, to truly live a well-balanced and happy life, which is consistent within itself and with our higher, spiritual nature, we must have pure thoughts.

> **"It is good to tame the mind, which is difficult to hold in and flighty, rushing wherever it listeth; a tamed mind brings happiness. Let the wise man guard his thoughts, for they are difficult to perceive,**

very artful, and they rush wherever they list: thoughts well guarded bring happiness."[33]

- Buddha, *The Dhammapada*, Ch. III, v. 35 – 36

How can this be achieved? Our intentions should be threefold: detachment from all things, good will towards all things, and harmlessness towards all things. These are the three things that should be our focus when dealing with others, or with the world at large, including the environment and animals. If we intend to detach ourselves, to renounce all that is ephemeral, then we are freeing ourselves from the cause of suffering. We abandon lust, idleness and delusion. If we have good will for all things, then we will help and truly love other human beings, we will care for and be compassionate to animals and other creatures, and we will care for the environment in which we live. Good will is all-embracing, like a river which has burst its banks. The water of good will flows over all things and encompasses all things. It is the basis of real love, which is attraction to the inner reality of things. If we develop an attitude of harmlessness, we will seek to avoid becoming the cause of suffering to others. We will endeavour to guard our speech, to avoid causing pain and try not to kill other creatures. We will become aware of the frivolity of killing animals for pleasure, and will no longer desire to harm others through anger or hatred.

3. Right speech

There are few things more dangerous than misuse of the faculty of speech. Speech can be an all-consuming fire, or it can be the source of guidance and wisdom. It has great potential both for good and for ill. Two of the greatest dangers when it comes to speech are backbiting and calumny. We should avoid talking badly about others when they are not present and we should also avoid slandering others. In general, we should not say anything negative about our fellow human beings, as negativity breeds negativity and leads to great harm—both to ourselves and others. As attractive as gossip and backbiting are, they are also gateways to suffering and attachment to the world. To be truly detached, we must avoid both practices. Likewise, we should avoid talking harshly to others, whether out of anger or malice, as words are like knives which cut into the hearts of man. Harsh words sever ties of friendship, break up marriages and lead to eternal regret and sorrow.

"Do not speak harshly to anybody; those who are spoken to will answer thee in the same way. Angry speech is painful, blows for blows will touch thee."[34]

- Buddha, *The Dhammapada*, Ch. X, v. 133

In order to avoid bad speech, we must cleave to good speech. That means we must praise one another, we must speak with kindliness and loving-kindness. We must say what is good and avoid saying what is evil. One of the best ways of doing this is through reading good words out loud. If we read a book of wisdom and cultivate the practise of reading excellent quotations from these writings out loud, the goodness of the words will gradually become natural and part of our every day practice. We need to make a concerted effort to avoid using swear words and expletives, which serve only to express ignorant attachment, and, instead, we must memorize and recite good and holy phrases and verses. Reading beautiful and inspiring poetry is also helpful in achieving this objective.

4. Right action (or behaviour)

Right action or behaviour is a central focus for all religions and philosophies. It is the essence of ethics and morality and the core of virtue. If we want to be good people and live in everlasting happiness, we must ensure that our deeds and actions are pure and good. We should endeavour not to harm others, nor to speak badly to others. We should avoid hurting others, abusing others, exploiting others, or otherwise doing wrongly to others. We should also cultivate kindness, consideration, tolerance, truthfulness, trustworthiness and compassion. Furthermore, we must live a morally-consistent life, which includes both morality in our day-to-day dealings with others, at home or in the workplace, on the street or in school, as well as in terms of our treatment of ourselves. We should avoid all sexual immorality and lust, as well as intoxication and mind-altering drugs. We should avoid any substances which cause lasting harm to the body, such as smoking, and overindulgence in compulsive activities.

"I praise good thoughts, good words, and good deeds and those that are to be thought, spoken, and done. I do accept all good thoughts, good words, and good deeds. I do renounce all evil thoughts, evil words, and evil deeds."[35]

- Zoroaster, *The Zend-Avesta*, Yasna – Introduction, v. 4.

Virtue is the essence of happiness. Too often, self-help books teach methods of achieving your inner potential or happiness, but they ignore the necessity of developing morally-consistent lives. We cannot ever be happy unless we are, first and foremost, honest. Truthfulness and trustworthiness are the foundation of all other virtues, as the Truth is the essence and foundation of right understanding. All other virtues are built upon this basic element. When we have developed truthfulness, we must live lives which are founded on piety. This means, firstly, that we must live clean lives, free from the consumption of alcohol and other intoxicants. Consumption of these substances may bring a temporary euphoria. However, ultimately, they are gateways to self-destruction and suffering.

"A virtue is that which both renders its possessor, as also his work, good. Hence we must say that every good act comes under virtue."[36]

- St. Thomas Aquinas, *On Prayer and the Contemplative Life*, Question LXXXI, II.

Secondly, we must avoid sexual misconduct, which means any sexual relations outside of marriage, which is an ancient institution created for the purpose of allowing an emotionally healthy and right expression of the sex drive, as well as for the procreation of children. Buddha says: "If man's desires flow unchecked, the waves of his lust and craving bear him off—misguided one!"[37] Sex outside of marriage, while popular in the modern, materialistic society in which we now live, is actually one of the main sources of discontent and suffering in our lives. Buddha exhorted his followers to avoid the 'ten evils', number 3 of which is described in the following words: "Abstain from impurity, and lead a life of chastity." [38] If we want to live truly happy lives, we should develop healthy relationships which are cultivated within the bonds of marriage. This will lead to long-term happiness and fulfilment. Forget about the past—now is the time to make adjustments to your

life that will bring about a happy and joyful life from
here on out.

"He whose evil deeds are covered by good deeds, brightens up this world, like the moon when freed from clouds."[39]
- Buddha, *The Dhammapada*, Ch. XIII, v. 173

Most importantly, our actions should be
beneficial to others. We should love others for the
sake of the souls within them, and for the sake of the
Creator which brought them into being. As such, we
should strive to do good for our fellow human beings
every day. We should endeavour to do good deeds,
such as giving to others, helping others, being kind to
others, sharing with others, advising others, and
giving love to others. It is only through love for others
that all the other virtues can be cultivated. Confucius
said: "It is only the (truly) virtuous man, who can love,
or who can hate, others."[40] What does this mean? We
can only truly love others if we follow a path of virtue.
And this love must be true and sincere, as Marcus
Aurelius opined: "Adapt thyself to the things with
which thy lot has been cast: and the men among
whom thou hast received thy portion, love them, but

do it truly, sincerely."[41] Sincere love for others is the way to practice right action.

5. Right livelihood (or living)

"Wealth and children are the adornment of this present life: but good works, which are lasting, are better in the sight of thy Lord as to recompense, and better as to hope."[42]
- Qur'ān 18:46

The fifth element of the Eightfold Path is right livelihood, or right living. This means having a good occupation which provides for the physical and material needs of life. We should, of course, find some way of supporting ourselves physically. Being idle or slothful is not really an option, as this would lead to a fruitless and pointless life. We cannot achieve happiness by remaining idle. Being requires doing, and doing is the essential outcome of being. If we are to be happy, we must be doing what makes ourselves and others happy. This means we should have a job or means of living which is consistent with our moral framework. Would it be acceptable to be an arms dealer, or a drug dealer? Would it be acceptable to sell sexual services? Would it be acceptable to make or serve alcohol? Would it be acceptable to promote the interests of the tobacco industry? Would it be acceptable to run a company which produces environmental damage and destruction? Would it be acceptable to exploit workers for the sake of profit and wealth? The answer to all of these is a resounding no. If we are to live happy and fulfilled lives, we need to have occupations which are morally acceptable, in order to live in accordance with virtue.

6. Right effort (or struggling)

"Fearlessness, singleness of soul, the will always to strive for wisdom; opened hand and governed appetites; and piety... humbleness, uprightness, heed to injure nought which lives, truthfulness, slowness unto wrath, a mind that lightly letteth go what others prize; and equanimity, and charity which spieth no man's faults; and tenderness towards all that suffer; a contented heart, fluttered by no desires; a bearing mind, modest, and grave... with patience, fortitude, and purity; an unrevengeful spirit... such be the signs, O Indian Prince! of him whose feet are set on that fair path which leads to heavenly birth!"[43]

- Krishna, *The Bhagavad-Gita*, Ch. XVI.

Effort is exertion. It means striving to achieve something. This is different from action in that action is merely *doing* something. Effort means exerting oneself in the achievement of a goal or object. Right effort, therefore, is striving to achieve that which is good. It is a form of wholesome energy which is expended when we try to achieve a good goal. For example, if we strive to bring about change for the better in our local communities, that is right effort. If we strive to bring about health and happiness for the poor who live in our neighbourhood, that is right effort. If we concentrate our energies on serving others, on doing that which is good, on providing vital services for others, then we are expending right effort. Diligence and exertion are also needed in perfecting ourselves and striving against the negative forces of materialism which surround us every day. It takes effort to be kind to others; it takes effort to avoid backbiting, gossip, calumny and white lies; it takes effort to avoid lust and sexual misconduct; it takes effort to look at our own faults instead of looking at the faults of others; it takes effort, furthermore, to purify our thoughts and intentions.

7. Right mindfulness

"And how, O king, is the Bhikshu[1] mindful and self-possessed?'

"In this matter, O king. The Bhikshu in going forth or in coming back keeps clearly before his mind's eye (all that is wrapt up therein--the immediate object of the act itself, its ethical significance, whether or not it is conducive to the high aim set before him, and the real facts underlying the mere phenomenon of the outward act). And so also in looking forward, or in looking round; in stretching forth his arm, or in drawing it in again; in eating or drinking, in masticating or swallowing, in obeying the calls of nature, in going or standing or sitting, in sleeping or waking, in speaking or in being still, he keeps himself aware of all it really means. Thus is it, O king, that the Bhikshu becomes mindful and self-possessed."[44]

- Buddha, *The Dîgha-Nikâya*, II. Sâmañña-Phala Sutta, v. 65, pp. 80 – 81.

Right mindfulness really means attentiveness or awareness of reality. It does not merely mean to be aware of one's physical surroundings, or to 'live in the

---

[1] A monk.

45

moment', as the catchphrase goes. It means, in one sense, to be aware of our inner and outer beings, as well as that which surrounds us. This means to be aware of every moment that passes, like waves on the sea. If we are mindful of ourselves, we must also be mindful of the presence of our Creator. Just as we have physical bodies that are ever-present within a physical setting, surrounded by air, water, earth and other elements, we are also eternal spirits which are illumined and sustained by a Higher Being which fills us with energy and power. True mindfulness, therefore, is to be aware of the presence of the Lord of all being—the Creative Force which engenders and moves all things both visible and invisible. Krishna says: "Higher still is He, the Highest, holding all, whose Name is LORD, the Eternal, Sovereign, First! Who fills all worlds, sustaining them."[45] This leads naturally to the next element of the Eightfold Path, which is meditation.

8. Right meditation (or contemplation)

Meditation is perhaps the most challenging concept for many of us, in this fast-paced world where there does not seem to be any time to sit down and commune with our spirits. Nevertheless, contemplation is what separates us from animals and this ability is the hallmark of human experience. It allows us to develop new inventions, to uncover new arts, and receive inspiration from a higher source or power. It is only in silence that we can find Truth, and only in contemplation that we can gain deeper and deeper insights and understanding. Thus does Jalālu'd-Dīn Rūmī, called Rumi, write in his *Dīvān-e-Shams-e-Tabrīzī*: "Be silent that the Lord who gave thee language may speak, for as He fashioned a door and lock, He has also made a key."[46] Meditation is the process of introspection, of communing with one's own inner being, of finding true silence and inner peace, being at one with oneself and the universe.

"These wise people, meditative, steady, always possessed of strong powers, attain to Nirvâna, the highest happiness."[47]
- Buddha, *The Dhammapada*, Ch. II, v. 23, p. 9.

There are many ways to meditate, but these almost always involve silence and solitude. It is best to meditate in a quiet place, away from distractions and noise. One way is to focus on a particular idea or concept, or a holy quotation or verse. This focus can lead us to understand inner meanings and depths of meaning hidden within that verse. Other methods of meditation include focussing on one's breathing or a particular physical object in order to melt away all desires and thoughts, until the mind is still and at peace, like a body of water that is still and smooth. This allows one to master one's own mind and control one's thoughts. Such meditation allows the inner voice to speak, the inner spirit—the soul—which, in turn, communes with the Higher Being which brought it into existence. Krishna, speaking as a Mouthpiece of that Creative Force, says: "Thou too, when heart and mind are fixed on Me, shalt surely come to Me!"[48]

Further practical steps related to meditation, and the other elements of the Eightfold Path, will be found in the next chapter.

Questions for Reflection

The following are some questions that will help us to reflect on what we have learned so far in this chapter:

1. Who should we turn to for guidance on the spiritual path?

2. What are the Four Noble Truths?

3. What is the Eightfold Path?

4. What is real love?

5. What is meditation?

∞∞∞∞∞∞∞∞∞∞∞∞∞∞∞∞∞∞∞∞∞∞∞∞∞∞

III. THE PATH OF VIRTUE – STEPS FOR FURTHER DEVELOPMENT

The following are some practical steps for further development on the path of detachment and virtue.

"Look upon the world as a bubble, look upon it as a mirage: the king of death does not see him who thus looks down upon the world."49

- Buddha, *The Dhammapada*, Ch. XIII, v. 170, p. 47

STEP 1 – RIGHT UNDERSTANDING

The practical step I would recommend at this stage is to make a conscious effort to notice the impermanence of reality. Every day, reflect on the nature of life and death and the changeability of all things. Reflect on your own mortality and the fleeting nature of the world. Do not be saddened or worried about death or loss, because both of these are part of the nature of material reality. Neither should cause you any alarm or worry. Realise that suffering comes from attachment and make a conscious effort to detach yourself. Make a concerted effort to be aware of the higher, noble nature within you. This is your soul. In short:

- Remain conscious of the impermanence of the material world

- Avoid grief or sorrow

- Detach yourselves from the physical world and other attachments

- Be aware of your inner nobility as an eternal, spiritual being

"All that we are is the result of what we have thought: it is founded on our thoughts, it is made up of our thoughts. If a man speaks or acts with a pure thought, happiness follows him, like a shadow that never leaves him."[50]

- Buddha, *The Dhammapada*, Chapter I, v. 2, p. 4.

STEP 2 – RIGHT THOUGHT

Try to focus your thoughts every day with the intention of doing good to others. Try to avoid thinking negatively. Read the quotations of the Buddha from this book and focus on them, as well as the other quotations above, including those from other sources, such as the Book of Proverbs, the New Testament and the Qur'ān. Let these teachings become the centre of your pattern of thinking. Try to avoid thinking negatively about others, thus avoiding hypocrisy and two-facedness. Try also to develop true love for all beings, which is, in reality, attraction to the inner reality of all things. Lastly, try to practise harmlessness by avoiding practices which harm other people, the environment or animals. Reducing or limiting your consumption of meat, poultry, fish, insects and other sentient creatures would be beneficial both for your body and your mind and would be consistent with compassion and the desire for harmlessness. In summary:

- Avoid negativity and negative thoughts about others

- Read quotations from the Buddha and other Teachers

- Love all living creatures by being attracted to their inner reality

- Practise non-violence and harmlessness by avoiding harm to others and the environment

- Reduce intake of meat and fish

"The Master said, 'The man of perfect virtue is cautious and slow in his speech.'"[51]

- Confucius, *Confucian Analects*, Book XII, Ch. III, v. 2.

STEP 3 – RIGHT SPEECH

Spend at least five minutes every day reading books of wisdom and beautiful poetry out loud. Find quotations from the Dhammapada, the Bible, the Bhagavad-Gita and the Qur'ān which you like or find inspiring and try to memorize them. Make repetition of these verses a part of your daily practice in the morning or evening. Try to learn some of the key quotations from this chapter, as well as from the Introduction and Chapter I. Make an attempt to learn quotations from subsequent chapters as well so that focusing on these will beautify your speech. When a thought of harshness or anger arises, remember the love that you feel for the person who is the cause of your anger. Remember that he or she is also a noble being full of eternal value and inner worth. Be attracted to that being by virtue of his or her inner reality and love him or her for the sake of the Creative Force which made them. Thus will you be able to avoid feeling hatred or enmity towards that person and will lose the desire to speak bad words to them, or about them in private or publicly. Love everyone as you would love your own self, or your family. In short:

- Spend five minutes every day reading books of wisdom and poetry

- Try to memorize inspirational quotations from the Dhammapada, Bible, Bhagavad-Gita and the Qur'ān. Repeat some of these every morning and evening.

- When you feel angry, remember your love for others and the inner worth of others

- Be attracted to others on account of the Creative Force which made them

- Love everyone as you would love your own self

"Right action consists in following those actions which are useful for happiness and avoiding those which lead to misery. The knowledge of these actions has been called practical knowledge."[52]

- Averroes (Ibn Rushd), *Philosophy*, I.

STEP 4 – RIGHT ACTION

First and foremost, abandon any unhealthy practices such as drinking alcohol and using drugs or other intoxicants. In the *Jātaka Tales*, we read: "He that drinks intoxicating liquors reels to and fro; he falls down precipices, into pools of water, and into the deep mire... Through the use of intoxicants, life is shortened, how then can he that is wise drink thereof?"[53] Likewise, in the *Dhammapada*, Buddha says: "And the man who gives himself to drinking intoxicating liquors, he, even in this world, digs up his own root."[54] In other words, by consuming intoxicants we harm the foundations of our well-being. If you are a smoker, try to give up smoking, step-by-step. Avoid taking part in a sexual relationship until after you are married. If married, remain faithful to your wife or husband. Try to do good unto others out of love for your fellow human beings. Be forbearing and tolerant of others and treat everyone you meet with kindliness and compassion, loving-kindness and mercy. Kindness to others is the essence of right action.

Right action is dependent on the development of virtue. Confucius said: "'If the will be set on virtue, there will be no practice of wickedness."[55] Try to focus on a different virtue every day, such as patience, tolerance, kindness, truthfulness, trustworthiness, compassion, fortitude, forbearance, equity, justice, etc. Here is a summary of some steps you should take:

- Avoid alcohol and other intoxicants
- Avoid smoking and other harmful behaviours
- Avoid stealing and lying
- Avoid sexual immorality and infidelity
- Be tolerant and forbearing of others
- Practise kindness and compassion to others
- Develop virtues every day

"**Whosoever has embraced this salvation, and gains a livelihood by unlawful means, when he eats the food and supports his life in any way that is blamed and disapproved by the Buddha, will find that there is no laughter and no joy for him.**"[56]

- Buddha, *Jātaka Tales*.

STEP 5 – RIGHT LIVING / LIVELIHOOD

Right livelihood means making a living in a morally-consistent way. We should earn our living in a way which does not conflict with the path of virtue and morality. For example, it would be morally inconsistent to earn a living through slavery or through enslaving others. It would morally inconsistent to work in a brewery or pub. Likewise, it would be morally inconsistent to earn a living through stealing, exploitation or piracy. Lying and deceit, intrigue and corruption, embezzlement and slander—all of these are wrong ways of living.

Right living includes doing a job which is of benefit to others or provides a service for others which does not violate moral principles. According to Buddha's teachings, there are five types of business which should be particularly avoided: the business of weapons, human beings (e.g. slavery), meat, intoxicants and poisons.[57] In the *Dîgha-Nikâya*, a Buddhist text, some thirty occupations are listed, but these mostly relate to palmistry, divination and other ways of foretelling the future.[58] To summarise:

- Ensure that your job or livelihood is morally consistent
- Avoid working in a situation which compromises your morality
- Avoid making or providing intoxicants (e.g. alcohol)
- Avoid any business related to exploitation of human beings (e.g. slavery, slave labour, human trafficking, pornography, prostitution, etc.)
- Avoid any business which relates to killing
- Avoid any business which is illegal or fundamentally immoral (e.g. stealing, piracy, corruption)

"By strenuous effort, by self-control, by temperance, let the wise man make for himself an island which the flood cannot overwhelm."[59]

- Buddha, *The Dhammapada*, v. 25, pp. 24 – 25.

STEP 6 – RIGHT EFFORT

Practising right effort essentially means focusing our efforts in the right direction. In particular, we must put effort into avoiding or preventing unwholesome qualities from developing, such as greed, anger, ignorance or lust. We must also make a concerted effort to extinguish those unwholesome qualities which have already developed within us. We must also endeavour to develop and cultivate good qualities, or virtues, which are the opposites of the bad qualities already mentioned, such as generosity, kindness, purity of heart and compassion. Lastly, we must try to strengthen and further develop those virtues which we already possess.[60] If we are kind already, we should make an effort to be even kinder.

It is not easy to put conscious effort into self-development. As Krishna states: "Of many thousand mortals, one, perchance, striveth for Truth; and of those few that strive—

Nay, and rise high—one only—here and there—knoweth Me, as I am, the very Truth."[61] The following is a summary:

- Strive to avoid bad qualities within yourself, such as greed, anger, ignorance and lust
- Strive to remove or extirpate existing bad qualities
- Strive to develop virtues, such as generosity, peacefulness, knowledge and detachment
- Strive to improve and enhance the virtues and good qualities that you already have
- Strive to attain knowledge and understanding of the Truth

∞∞∞∞∞∞∞∞∞∞∞∞∞∞∞∞∞∞∞∞∞∞∞

"A priest, in walking thoroughly comprehends his walking, and in standing thoroughly comprehends his standing, and in sitting thoroughly comprehends his sitting, and in lying down thoroughly comprehends his lying down, and in whatever state his body may be thoroughly comprehends that state."[62]

- *Mahâ-Satipatthāna-Sutta*, pp. 357 – 358.

STEP 7 – RIGHT MINDFULNESS

As we learned in the previous chapter, mindfulness is awareness of oneself and one's surroundings, as well as a higher awareness of the reality of things. It is being constantly aware of the nature of existence, and the impermanence of all that surrounds us. In the quotation above, from the *Mahâ-Satipatthāna-Sutta*, the example is given of a priest who, while walking remains conscious of his walking, while standing remains conscious of his standing, and so on. Whatever his state or his surroundings, he tries to remain conscious and aware of the moment. Not only is he aware, but he thoroughly comprehends the reality of that state. For example, he understands that the physical body he is in will eventually die and is impermanent, while his eternal soul is ever-present and eternal. Furthermore, by being mindful of others and their essential nobility, we are able to be compassionate to others. The following are some steps to take:

- Be conscious and aware of your daily activities, your movement and surroundings
- Be aware of the impermanence of everything around you
- Remember the essential nobility of all human beings
- Remember the spiritual nature of your inner being

"The Saint who shuts outside his placid soul all touch of sense, letting no contact through; whose quiet eyes gaze straight from fixed brows, whose outward breath and inward breath are drawn, equal and slow through nostrils still and close; that one—with organs, heart, and mind constrained, bent on deliverance, having put away passion, and fear, and rage;— hath, even now, obtained deliverance, ever and ever freed."[63]

- Krishna, *The Bhagavad-Gita*, Ch. V.

STEP 8 – RIGHT CONTEMPLATION

Contemplation or meditation is a great way of freeing your mind from worry and cares. It is a method for self-purification and developing insights. One method is given in the Bhagavad-Gita, as quoted above. It is recommended that one first detach oneself from 'all touch of sense', i.e. attachment to physical world. Elsewhere, Krishna says: "Sequestered should he sit, steadfastly meditating, solitary, his thoughts controlled, his passions laid away, quit of belongings."[64] Sequestered, here, means isolated and away from the noise and hubbub of life. It would be a good idea, therefore, to find a quiet and secluded place, such as one's bedroom or garden, or an isolated spot in the woods or countryside, where one is unlikely to be disturbed by the noise and confusion of the modern, materialistic civilization we all live in. One should remain seated on the ground, perhaps on a mat, sitting up straight. It is customary to sit with crossed legs, though this is not strictly necessary. One could equally sit on a chair or cushion. Next, one concentrates on one's breathing, being aware of each breath, breathing deeply through the nose and releasing. One's meditation should be 'bent on deliverance', i.e. done with the goal of obtaining spirituality and higher awareness, free from the attachments of the material world.

Other methods of concentration and meditation include reading or chanting verses, or mantras, and focusing on the words. This can be done through repetition of the same verse or using different verses. In summary:

- In order to meditate, find a quiet and secluded place, or your bedroom
- Concentrate on your breathing, using deep breaths
- Focus your meditation on achieving a higher level of spiritual awareness
- Read verses aloud in order to focus on their sound and meaning

Questions for Reflection:

The following are some questions that will help us to reflect on what we have learned so far in this chapter:

1. What are some practices for right understanding, right thought and right speech?
2. What is right action and what behaviours should be avoided? What is right livelihood?
3. What is right effort and what should we strive for?
4. What is right mindfulness and how can we practise it?
5. What are some ways to practise meditation?
6. In the next chapter, we will learn about the Second Way to Be – Radiant Acquiescence.

∞∞∞∞∞∞∞∞∞∞∞∞∞∞∞∞∞∞∞∞∞∞∞∞

IV. THE SECOND WAY TO BE – RADIANT ACQUIESCENCE

Parable

"I saw on the sea-shore a holy man who had been torn by a tiger, and could get no salve to heal his wound. For a length of time he suffered much pain, and was all along offering thanks to the Most High. They asked him, saying, 'Why are you so grateful?' He answered, 'God be praised that I am overtaken with misfortune and not with sin! Were that beloved friend, God, to give me over to death, take heed, and think not that I should be solicitous about life. I would ask, What hast thou seen amiss in thy poor servant that thy heart should take offence at me? for that could alone give me a moment's uneasiness.'"[65]

- Saadi, *The Gulistan*, CH II, XII.

Reflections

In the parable above from the *Gulistān* ('rose-garden') of Saadi, a famous Persian poet from the city of Shiraz in Iran, we see a true example of radiant

66

acquiescence. The holy man, although bitten by a tiger, and certainly suffering in the realm of the body, was praising God that he was not suffering from sin. Sin means to commit acts which are against virtue and are not morally consistent. It may be regarded as the opposite of virtue. He was grateful to God because he knew that true misfortune was to have a bad character and bad behaviour, while true happiness was to have a virtuous character and develop the love of God in his heart. He accepted God's Will for his life radiantly and joyfully. He was detached from the material condition, even though he still experienced it, because he had an awareness that whatever happened to him was in accordance with the Primal Will, which is the moving force behind all things. To be truly happy is to live one's life in accordance to this mighty Force, submitting oneself to its way and purpose.

To acquiesce means to submit or accept silently and without protest. It is sometimes put into a negative context of accepting reluctantly. The meaning that we intend, however, is willing acceptance and submission. The word 'radiant' implies shining and glowing. **Radiant**

acquiescence, then, means accepting and submitting with abundant joyfulness and radiance, knowing that such submission is the best wisdom. Radiant acquiescence means submission not just to *any* being or will, but to the Divine Being—the Primal Will which brought the universe—and all that is within it—into existence.

It is a difficult concept for many, in this modern world of material advancement and scientific development, to accept the existence of a Divine Being—a Higher Power above and beyond the whole of existence. But this reluctance stems from a fundamental misunderstanding—the idea that this Being, or God, is part of the material world. Arguments about first causes and creation *ex nihilo* ('out of nothing'), etc. all imply causation within a single plane of reality. The idea, which is refuted by many, is that God is a sort of material energy or being which causes everything else to come into existence— this is a magical and irrational conception.

Rather, I would argue that such arguments are completely irrelevant, as the Divine Being is entirely transcendent above the realm of material existence. Some scientists believe that the material world is all that exists, and perhaps this universe, they argue, is one among many in a limitless multiverse. But all these universes of which they conceive are extensions of the same plane of existence—the plane of the material world. The ultimate Reality—which is God—exists in a realm so exalted and inaccessible that the nature of its existence is beyond human conception. There are realities far greater than the material world, such as the afterlife, and the realm of the soul, which is far beyond the level of material existence, though there is a relationship between the two realms. Nevertheless, the human being is fundamentally a spiritual being which relies upon divine inspiration and mercy for its growth and development.

"There is, O monks, a state where there is neither earth, nor water, nor heat, nor air; neither infinity of space nor infinity of consciousness, nor nothingness, nor perception nor non-perception; neither this world nor that world, neither sun nor moon. It is the uncreate."[66]

- Buddha, *The Gospel of Buddha*, XXVI., p. 81

To attain true happiness, therefore, we must be content with the Primal Will, which is the Way of the universe. The Primal Will may be said to be that Active Force which originates from the Divine Being and which brings all of creation into existence. It may be considered to be a Lamp which shines throughout all time, without beginning or end. The material and spiritual realms of existence—the whole of creation—may be regarded as the light which emits from the Lamp. Creation is dependent upon its Source, which is the Primal Will, so it may be called contingent. We are all rays of light from that Lamp and are made in its image, being imbued with the qualities or attributes of the Lamp. In other words, the virtues and qualities which we are trying to acquire are the virtues and qualities of the Primal Will, which Itself is generated by the Divine Being. The Chinese sage, Laozi, refers to the Primal Will as the Tao (or the 'Way'). He says: "The relation of the Tao to all the world is like that of the great rivers and seas to the streams from the valleys."[67] He also says that it "produces (all things) and nourishes them."[68]

"All things are produced by the Tao, and nourished by its outflowing operation. They receive their forms according to the nature of each, and are completed according to the circumstances of their condition. Therefore all things without exception honour the Tao, and exalt its outflowing operation."[69]

- Laozi, *The Tao Teh Ching*, Part II, 51.1.

We all exist through the limitless power and unceasing radiance of the Primal Will, which is at the heart of all existence, even though its own existence is beyond the realm of the material world. It is like the heart of creation, even though it exists beyond time and space. It is the Source of all love and energy, even though it exists beyond even the realm of names and definitions. The qualities and attributes of that Primal Being are infused into every atom of existence. In everything that exists, we can see a reflection or a manifestation of those attributes. In human beings *uniquely*, however, is the capacity to develop *all* of these attributes, as we are created in the image of our Creator. As noble, spiritual beings, we are invested with great power and potential. Each one of us is a truly splendid and magnificent being, but we are not even aware of our own reality. We are too locked up within the cage of ego and passion, lust and material desires, that we do not recognise the higher self within. It is only by bringing our higher selves into submission to the ultimate Primal Will that we can achieve our purpose in life, which is to know that Higher Power and draw near unto It.

"Then is God perfectly simple and true both in word and deed; he changes not; he deceives not, either by sign or word, by dream or waking vision."[70]
- Plato, *The Republic*, Book II.

Radiant acquiescence is developed by, first of all, acknowledging the reality of the Divine Being and, secondly, by accepting whatever that Being has willed for our lives. This means accepting whatever befalls us, whether good or ill, without complaint, and with joyful acceptance. It also means accepting whatever way that Being has prescribed for us to live, through the development of virtues and divine perfections. How can we know what way that Being wants us to live? We certainly cannot know it purely from our own intuition. As we have mentioned earlier, it is only by turning to those Perfect Teachers who have come throughout the ages to bring us messages of Truth, and prescriptions for living, that we can understand the way that we should live. These include Zoroaster, Krishna, Buddha and Christ, whom we have already cited in preceding chapters. Other teachers there are who have also come to a glimmering of understanding of the Truth, though to a lesser degree than these Perfect Teachers. These other teachers include Laozi, Confucius and many others.

Gautama Buddha gives the parable of the elephant as a means of understanding how to be truly acquiescent to God's Will. The elephant is the embodiment of patience and true submission to the Primal Will. The parable is described in the *Dhammapada*, which contains the core of his teachings:

"Silently shall I endure abuse as the elephant in battle endures the arrow sent from the bow: for the world is ill-natured. They lead a tamed elephant to battle, the king mounts a tamed elephant; the tamed is the best among men, he who silently endures abuse. Mules are good, if tamed, and noble Sindhu horses, and elephants

with large tusks; but he who tames himself is better still. For with these animals does no man reach the untrodden country (Nirvâna), where a tamed man goes on a tamed animal, viz. on his own well-tamed self."[71]

- Buddha, *The Dhammapada*, Ch. XXIII, v. 320 – 324

This same virtue of acquiescence is described in the Gospels, including the Gospel of Matthew. Famously, Jesus Christ preached that, on a personal level, one should not resist evil. One should accept persecution and abuse and return loving-kindness instead. This is the ultimate essence of submission to the Will of God. He is recorded to have said:

"Ye have heard that it hath been said, An eye for an eye, and a tooth for a tooth: But I say unto you, That ye resist not evil: but whosoever shall smite thee on thy right cheek, turn to him the other also. And if any man will sue thee at the law, and take away thy coat, let him have thy cloak also. And whosoever shall compel thee to go a mile, go with him twain. Give to him that asketh thee, and from him that would borrow of thee turn not thou away. Ye have heard that it hath been said, Thou shalt love thy neighbour, and hate thine enemy.

But I say unto you, Love your enemies, bless them that curse you, do good to them that hate you, and pray for them which despitefully use you, and persecute you; That ye may be the children of your Father which is in heaven: for he maketh his sun to rise on the evil and on the good, and sendeth rain on the just and on the unjust."[72]

- Jesus Christ, Matthew 5:43 – 45

We can clearly see here that there is no difference between the teachings of Gautama Buddha and Jesus Christ on this matter. We must accept not only whatever happens in our life, but we must also return good for evil, not evil for good. Revenge, hatred and animosity serve no purpose. There is no need to 'get back at' anyone. When we hurt others, we bring yet more negativity into the world. When we love others, and are forbearing and patient, we bring love into the world and serve the purpose for which we were created.

We should remember that our spiritual reality is ever-present, and that our hearts are thrones for the Will of God to manifest Itself within us. The Muslim philosopher, Al-Ghazālī, in his famous book, *The*

Alchemy of Happiness, has written: "Some idea of the reality of the heart, or spirit, may be obtained by a man closing his eyes and forgetting everything around except his individuality. He will thus also obtain a glimpse of the unending nature of that individuality."[73] True knowledge, then, is realization of the reality of the soul within each one of us and the Higher Being which created us. To acknowledge and accept this Higher Being is called belief. In the Bhagavad-Gita, Krishna explains: "There is no purifier like thereto in all this world, and he who seeketh it shall find it—being grown perfect—in himself. Believing, he receives it when the soul masters itself, and cleaves to Truth, and comes—possessing knowledge—to the higher peace, the uttermost repose."[74] Meditation is useful in reaching this level of awareness.

The concepts mentioned in this chapter are, on first examination, somewhat complex. However, by re-reading the chapter and focusing on the quotations, we can come to a better understanding of the meaning of radiant acquiescence and the concepts of the Divine Being and Primal Will.

Questions for Reflection:

The following are some questions that will help us to reflect on what we have learned so far in this chapter:

1. What does radiant acquiescence mean?
2. What brings creation into being and sustains it?
3. What is the Primal Will?
4. What do human beings have the capacity to do?
5. How should we react to negativity, persecution and hatred?

∞∞∞∞∞∞∞∞∞∞∞∞∞∞∞∞∞∞∞∞∞∞∞∞∞

V. THE SECOND PRACTICE – PRAYER:

"He is within all beings—and without—
motionless, yet still moving; not discerned
for subtlety of instant presence; close to
all, to each; yet measurelessly far! Not
manifold, and yet subsisting still in all
which lives; for ever to be known as the
Sustainer, yet, at the End of Times, He
maketh all to end—and re-creates. The
Light of Lights He is, in the heart of the
Dark, shining eternally. Wisdom He is and
Wisdom's way, and Guide of all the wise,
planted in every heart."[75]

- Krishna, *The Bhagavad-Gita*, Ch. XIII.

Remember: we have now set foot on a path to
eternity, a path which has no end, but the goal of
which is ultimate Truth and Reality. We have learned
about acquiring virtues and being detached from the
material world. We have also learned about the
principle of radiant acquiescence, which means
accepting and embracing the Divine Will as our own
will. We subjugate our own selfish desires and ego for
that of the Primal Will, which generates and sustains

the whole of existence, which Laozi refers to as the Tao, and Buddha refers to as the Unoriginated, the Uncreated, the Unborn. We must now consider how to develop this quality of radiant acquiescence, so that we may live our lives in accordance with the Will of our Creator and, step-by-step and pace-by-pace, we may develop the divine attributes and qualities, until we are ready to ascend from the world of material things unto the higher world—the spiritual kingdom— which exists outside of this physical universe but is, nevertheless, intimately connected with it.

In order to achieve oneness with the Divine Will, we must practise prayer. Prayer means communion with the Divine Being. It is not conversation with some outside creature which exists far away in a glorious heaven. Rather, it means looking within ourselves and making contact with our own souls, which are the mirrors of the Primal Will. God is the source of love and perfection, and it is only by looking within our own selves that we may find that love and perfection and commune with the Source of all power and might. We must become like receivers which pick up the divine signal, and bowls which receive the water of life, which springs up from the Wellspring of eternity. Like canals dug deep within the ground, we must connect ourselves with the ocean of eternal wisdom, which will flow through us with everlasting torrents of wisdom and understanding. We cannot have the strength to withstand the pain and suffering of the material world unless we tap into the Source of absolute power, which is accessible to all. There is nothing preventing us from tapping into that power, except our own unwillingness to embrace it.

"It is not so much a question whether we are to pray by words or deeds as whether we are to pray at all if God already knows what is needful for us. Yet the very giving ourselves to prayer has the effect of soothing our minds and purifying them; it makes us more fit to receive the Divine gifts which are spiritually poured out upon us."[76]
- St. Thomas Aquinas, On Prayer and the Contemplative Life, LXXXIII.

The first step in prayer is to turn our inner selves towards the Divine Being. We do that by shutting out our thoughts and desires, calming ourselves, and taking on an attitude of reverence. Reverence is a form of respect for that which is higher. It involves dressing appropriately, being physically clean and in a calm state of being. It means moving gracefully, sitting serenely, and generally behaving with decency and decorum.

When we are in this state of receptivity, we should then call upon our Creator and ask Him whatever we need. This could be physical needs, such as food, water and shelter. However, the highest prayer is to ask for our will to be in conformity with the Divine Will and for God to act through us, guiding and inspiring us in all our pursuits. If we ask for physical things, our prayers may be answered, especially if they are urgent prayers for help. However, they may also go unanswered, as God gives us what we truly *need*, not always what we *desire*. The highest prayer, however, will *always* be answered, if we are sincere and steadfast in our determination.

In particular, there are some prayers which exist either in ancient scriptures or in the writings of saints and Prophets which are particularly helpful in helping us to focus our energies on communion with God and contemplation of His attributes and qualities. These written prayers help us to channel that divine power within us which can then manifest itself in the form of spiritual power and inspiration. However, it should be remembered that merely reading words has no effect. Reading is the outer action, which must be accompanied by the inner action, which is turning one's heart to God. The outer body, also, should practise reverence while praying. We should also practise respect for others while they are praying. The following are some examples of prayers which we can say:

Prayers from various Holy Writings

"The LORD is my light and my salvation; whom shall I fear? the LORD is the strength of my life; of whom shall I be afraid?"

- Psalm 27:1

"Have mercy upon me, O God, according to thy lovingkindness: according unto the multitude of thy tender mercies blot out my transgressions. Wash me thoroughly from mine iniquity, and cleanse me from my sin."

- Psalm 51:1 – 2

"Create in me a clean heart, O God and renew a right spirit within me."

- Psalm 51:10

"Our Father which art in heaven, Hallowed be thy name. Thy kingdom come. Thy will be done in earth, as it is in heaven. Give us this day our daily bread. And forgive us our debts, as we forgive our debtors. And lead us not into temptation, but deliver us from evil."

- Matthew 6:9 – 13

"In the Name of God, the Compassionate, the Merciful!

PRAISE be to God, Lord of the worlds!

The Compassionate, the Merciful!

King on the day of reckoning!

Thee only do we worship, and to Thee do we cry for help.

Guide Thou us on the straight path,

The path of those to whom Thou hast been gracious;–with whom thou art not angry, and who go not astray."

- Qur'ān 1:1 - 7

"Say rather, 'O my Lord, increase knowledge unto me.'"

- Qur'ān 20:114

"Praises, and songs, and adorations do we offer to the Lord All-Wise,[77] and to Righteousness the Best; yea, we offer and we ascribe them, and proclaim them. And to Thy good Kingdom, O Lord All-Wise! may we attain for ever, and a good King be Thou over us; and let each man of us, and so each woman, thus abide, O Thou most beneficent of beings, and for both the worlds!"[78]

- Zoroaster, *The Avesta*, Yasna Haptanghaiti (Worship in Seven Chapters), 41.1-2

"Worthily, Lord of Might! the whole world hath delight in Thy surpassing power, obeying Thee... Thou, of all souls the Soul! the Comprehending Whole! of being formed, and formless being the Framer; O Utmost One! O Lord! older than eld, Who stored the worlds with wealth of life! O Treasure-Claimer, Who wottest all, and art Wisdom Thyself!... Again, Thou God! again a thousand thousand times be magnified!... For Thou art, now I know, Father of all below, of all above, of all the worlds within. "[79]

- Prayer of Arjuna, *The Bhagavad-Gita*, Ch. XI.

These prayers, being revealed in the scriptures of old, are imbued with a certain power and influence which our own, individual prayers are incapable of expressing. However, remember that ritualism is not conducive to real spirituality. Therefore, do not simply repeat prayers for the sake of repeating them. Try to feel and mean each word as you say them.

Furthermore, it is not enough to simply dedicate a certain amount of prayer every day. We must also try to live in a state of prayer. This means to live in a constant state of supplication and prayer to God within ourselves. Whenever we go anywhere, we pray that God will protect us. Whenever we are ill, we pray that God will heal us. Whenever we are late, we pray that God will assist us. Whenever we are tired, we pray that God will give us rest. Whenever we commit sins or fall short of the straight path, we ask God to guide us on the straight path. Thus, at each and every moment, we are recognising our dependency on the Higher Power which sustains us. Thus we develop the attribute of radiant acquiescence, which acknowledges that essential dependency on God.

"Pray in this wise and allay your difficulties;

'Give us good in the house of our present world,

And give us good in the house of our next world.

Make our path pleasant as a garden,

And be Thou, O Holy One, our goal!'"[80]

- Jalālu'd-Dīn Rūmī, *The Masnavī*, Book II, Story X.

Prayer should be cultivated on a daily basis. It is not something which we should only do when we are suffering or in pain. Like a medicine, it should be practised at certain times every day, e.g. at dawn, in the morning and evening, or at midday or midnight. "The taint of prayers," says Buddha, "is non-repetition."[81] Whichever times you choose, make sure to make prayer a regular practice which can revitalize your energies every day and allow you to achieve your inner potential and inner peace. The Book of Psalms in the Bible is a particularly good source of prayers and supplications, which have been recited and used for thousands of years. The Lord's Prayer, from the Gospel of Matthew, as cited above, is also highly recommended, as Jesus gives this as a template for how we should pray. In that prayer, we praise the Divine Being, ask for His kingdom to come and for His Will to be fulfilled on earth as it is in the heaven of His decree. We also ask for our daily needs, here referred to as 'daily bread', and ask for forgiveness for ourselves and those who have wronged us, including our enemies. Lastly, we ask to be kept on the straight path and led away from errors.

Another widely used and significant prayer is called *al-Fātihah* (lit. 'The Opening'), which is the first *sūrah* (or 'chapter') of the Qur'ān, revealed by the Prophet Muhammad. The message of the prayer is largely similar to the Lord's Prayer. God is invoked by His attributes of mercy and compassion. Second, we praise God as the Lord of the worlds. Third, we again invoke His mercy and compassion. Next, He is invoked as the 'King' of the Day of Reckoning, i.e. the day of fulfilment, when everything reaches its consummation. Lastly, we ask to be guided on the Straight Path, which is the Middle Way of the Buddha. This is the path of those who have turned their inner beings towards their Creator and are attuned with His Will, rather than following the path of those who have turned away from the Divine Will and chosen to follow their own selfish passions and ego. This prayer is recited several times within each of the five daily prayers practised within Islam. Mere recitation of the prayer, however, is fruitless, unless the recitation is accompanied by understanding, reverence and the intention to communicate with the Creative Force which embraces all things.

Questions for Reflection:

The following are some questions that will help us to reflect on what we have learned so far in this chapter:

1. What is the second practice and what does it mean?
2. Give an example of a prayer quoted above.
3. How often should we pray?
4. What do we ask for in the Lord's Prayer?
5. What do we ask for in *al-Fātihah* (the opening chapter of the Qur'ān)?

∞∞∞∞∞∞∞∞∞∞∞∞∞∞∞∞∞∞∞∞∞∞∞∞∞

VI. PRAYER – STEPS FOR FURTHER DEVELOPMENT

The following are some practical steps for further development in the practice of prayer and supplication to the Divine Being.

> **"O Moses! verily, I am thy Lord, so take off thy sandals; verily, thou art in the holy valley Tuwâ, and I have chosen thee. So listen to what is inspired thee; verily, I am God, there is no god but Me! then serve Me, and be steadfast in prayer to remember Me."[82]**
>
> - Qur'ān 20:12 – 14[83]

STEP 1 – CLEANLINESS & REVERENCE

In order to have a clean mind, the first step is to clean one's body. The body is the lamp through which the light of the soul shines. Therefore, as we turn our minds and hearts to the Divine Essence and the higher nature within us, we must cleanse our bodies and ensure that we are physically clean and pure. In developing the right posture of reverence, we should dress appropriately, wearing clean and unstained clothing, dressing modestly and appropriately. We should comb our hair and find a clean and quiet spot to pray. One can pray standing or sitting, or even while walking or pacing back and forth. If we are sitting, we can use a chair or sit on the floor. When seated on the floor, a prayer rug is recommended, as this provides a clean space on which to sit and, if one wishes, to prostrate oneself to the Creator who made us. Cleanliness means cleanness of body, clothing, mind and soul.

"It was said by a pious man, 'Cleanliness is next to godliness.'"[84]

- John Wesley, *Sermons on Several Occasions*, Sermon XCVIII.

The next step is to ensure that we have a reverent attitude to the Divine and maintain a reverent posture. We should sit with respect and dignity, or stand with a straight back and firm poise. We should imagine that we are in the presence of the King of the universe, who is ever-present yet eternally transcendent. How would we behave if we were introduced to the Queen of Great Britain? How much more reverent would we be if we were to enter the presence of the King of Kings—the Ruler over all that is, has been and ever will be? It is with this attitude of utter submission and respect that we should approach prayer. We must focus ourselves on our objective of supplicating the King of the universe and clear our minds of all things else.

> **"The primary and fundamental purity is that of the soul, and so with impurity. You cannot find the same impurity in a soul as in a body: the soul's impurity you will find to be just this—that which renders it unclean for its own functions... The soul's impurity consists in bad judgements, and purification consists in producing in it right judgements, and the pure soul is one which has right judgements, for this alone is proof against confusion and pollution in its functions. And one ought to endeavour, as far as may be, to achieve a similar cleanliness in one's body too."**[85]

- Epictetus, The Discourses of Epictetus, Chapter XI.

Purity of body and purity of mind are intertwined. We should clear our minds of all impure thoughts and desires, and all traces of prejudice and hatred, filling our souls with the water of love and focusing on the eternal love which flows through us, like water issuing from a river into a tributary. We must empty ourselves of self and passion and embrace the higher nature within us. The following is a summary:

- Wash and cleanse yourself so that you are clean
- Wear clean, dignified and modest clothes and comb your hair
- Find a clean and quiet place to sit, stand or walk while praying
- Stand or sit appropriately with a firm posture
- Adopt an attitude of reverence
- Purify your mind from impure thoughts and desires

"When thou enterest into prayer in sincerity, thou wilt come forth from prayer with all thy desire obtained; but if without sincerity thou offer a hundred salutations, thou art still a bungler, thy work a failure. One salutation is the same as two hundred, one prostration in sincerity is worth thy standing erect a hundred times, for the

prayer that is mere matter of custom is dust that is scattered by the wind. The prayers that reach God's court are those that the soul prays; the mere mimic is ever a mendicant, praying unworthily, without intelligence, since he chooses the path of folly. For on this path prayer of the spirit is of more account than barren mimicry."[86]

- Sanā'ī, *The Hadîqatu'l-Haqîqat*, pp. 116 – 117.

STEP 2 – SINCERITY & INTENT

Prayer is not merely a series of words uttered by your mouth, or even a series of thoughts issuing from your conscious mind. Rather, prayer depends, first and foremost, on sincerity and the intent to commune with God. Before praying, make a firm intention within yourself to communicate with the Creative Force which generates and sustains the universe. Then, sincerely and intently pray to that Divine Being. Make mention of the Name of God to help you focus yourself on His Essence. In short:

- Sincerely desire to commune with God
- Intend to communicate with the Divine Being

- Make mention of the Name of God to help you focus on His Being and Essence

"Thou art secure when thou pronouncest His name,—thou keepest a firm footing on thy path; make thou thy tongue moist, like earth, with remembrance of Him, that He may fill thy mouth, like the rose, with gold. He fills with life the soul of the wise man; the heart of the lover of self He leaves thirsty."[87]

- Sanā'ī, *The Hadîqatu'l-Haqîqat*, p. 47.

STEP 3 – PRAISING THE DIVINE BEING

Praise of God may seem strange at first, if one is unused to praying. However, it becomes habitual over time. Does God need our praise? No. Nevertheless, praising and glorifying God is essential to developing an attitude of prayer. It is a sign of gratitude and thankfulness, which are attributes of God. We should remember all that God has done for us, bringing us into existence, feeding and clothing us, providing opportunities to follow a spiritual path. Even the fact that this book has come into your hands, or was purchased and downloaded on your e-book reader, is something to be thankful for. Any word of guidance we receive, any help we are given along the Path to Truth is something to appreciate. We are always thankful to those who help us. Should we not also be thankful to that Higher Being which loves us more than we love our own selves—which created us because of His eternal love for us and which gave us immortality and eternal existence? He has given us opportunities to progress eternally and to develop abiding happiness and joy. We should praise God by calling upon His names and attributes and thanking Him for everything we have received. In short:

- We should always praise God, as this is essential to an attitude of prayer
- Praising God is a sign of our gratitude and thankfulness for all that He has given us
- We should be thankful for all the things in our lives, including material goods, spirituality and guidance
- We should be thankful to God because of His eternal love for us and the gift of everlasting life and eternal progress

- We should be thankful because God has given us the keys to abiding joy and happiness
- We should praise God by calling upon His attributes

"The men of the Path walk in trust; if thou has a constant trust in Him, why not also in His feeding thee? Bring then thy belongings to the street of trust in God; then fortune will come out to meet thee." [88]

- Sanā'ī, *The Hadîqatu'l-Haqîqat*, p. 81.

STEP 4 – ASKING FOR OUR NEEDS AND WISHES

We should, of course, be fully reliant and dependent on the Creative Force which brought us into being. Even as our very existence has depended upon God, so should we depend on God for our material needs and everything else that we need. This does not mean we should sit idly and let God give us everything we need. On the contrary, we should work for our living and use the excess of our earnings to help others and better humanity. What we are saying here is that we must have complete trust in and reliance on God. We should trust God and have faith that He will feed us, give us our basic necessities and provide all that we truly need. He gives us life and He gives us death. He gives us sickness and healing. St. Paul wrote: "And all things are of God."[89] And in the Qur'ān, God says—glorified be He: "He maketh alive and He causeth to die, and to Him shall ye return."[90]

In all things, we should rely on God and accept whatever He has given us or will give us. If we are ill, we should pray for healing. If we are poor, we should pray for sustenance. If we are ignorant, we should pray for knowledge. If we are sad, we should pray for happiness. However irrational this may seem to the rationalist, the proof of the pudding is in the eating. When we are totally reliant and dependent on God, we begin to feel blessed and our lives become a series of blessings and tests, tests and blessings, as difficulties become opportunities for growth and good-fortunes become bounties from God. As it is written in the Qur'ān: "And put thy trust in God: for He is the Hearing, the Knowing."[91] This is how to lead a miraculous and abundant life. In short:

- We should be totally reliant on God for all our needs

- We should work to support ourselves but trust in God
- We should be aware that all things come from God
- We should see troubles and difficulties as tests and good-fortune as a blessing and bounty
- This will help us to feel blessed

"The souls illuminated take that road which hath no turning back—their sins flung off by strength of faith." [92]

- Krishna, *The Bhagavad-Gita*, Ch. V.

STEP 5 – ASKING FOR FORGIVENESS

When praying, we should ask our Creator for forgiveness. We should not see this in the overly literalist sense of trying to erase sins, as if we all have a sin counter which tolls the number of sins we have committed each day. Rather, we should recognise our shortcomings, ask for the spiritual effects of those shortcomings to be cleansed and washed away, and ask for guidance in living a more morally-consistent and virtuous life. This is a more holistic way of looking at the concept of sin and forgiveness. It is not a case of merely trying to make up for one's wrongs. It is a way of trying to heal one's own soul and then improve, starting from a clean slate. The way to truly achieve forgiveness is with genuine contrition and a desire to do what is right. We should endeavour to develop virtues and avoid vices within us and try to do what is right. Only with reformation of character and a sincere desire to change can this be fully achieved. In summary:

- We should recognise our own shortcomings and ask God for forgiveness
- We should see this as a way of healing our own souls
- Forgiveness allows us to start again with a clean slate
- We can only achieve forgiveness if we have genuine contrition and sincerity
- We should try to reform our characters, develop virtues and avoid vices

"When the decree of God becomes the pleasure of man,

Then man desires the fulfilment of God's decrees;

And this too spontaneously, not in hope of reward,

But because his very nature is congruous therewith."93

- Jalālu'd-Dīn Rūmī, *The Masnavī*, Book III, Story XI.

STEP 6 – ASKING FOR THE DIVINE WILL

We are now moving closer and closer to the goal of prayer, which is to align our inner and outer beings with the Way of the universe, with our ultimate purpose and the Pre-existent Will of God. There is no goal higher than to live according to the Divine Will. There is no higher purpose than to wish for and live according to that Will. It is an impossible task to fully and completely live in line with the Divine Will. Only those great Teachers who have completely manifested the divine attributes, such as Moses and Zoroaster, Krishna and Buddha, Jesus and Muhammad, have attained to so high a station. Nevertheless, we should all try to achieve what we are capable of and every human being has a degree of spiritual capacity. The capacity of one person may be a small cupful of divine grace and wisdom. Yet another may have the capacity of a carafe, while another more may have the capacity of a ewer. We all have varying capacities, but we are all capable of receiving divine grace and power.

What we should do is to ask God to align our wills to His, as we are incapable of doing so without divine assistance. By submitting ourselves to His Will, we open up the door to divine grace. If we have the intent to abide by His Will, God will help us to achieve our goal. We should strive, day-by-day to change our attitudes, beliefs and behaviours, in order to bring them closer to the teachings of wisdom and understanding, as expressed in the scriptures of the world. Some practical ways to achieve are as follows:

- Pray for our wills to be aligned to the Divine Will
- Pray for divine inspiration and guidance, expecting God to fulfil your wish
- Act as if the prayer has been answered and act accordingly
- Trust in God that whatever He wills will come to pass

"And celebrate the praise of thy Lord before the sunrise, and before its setting; and some time in the night do thou praise him, and in the extremes of the day, that thou haply mayest please Him."[94]

- Qur'ān 20:130

STEP 7 – MAKING PRAYER A DAILY PRACTICE

It is essential to pray every day in order to develop a habit of spiritual practice. Prayer is not something to be taken lightly or ignored lightly. It is an essential practice for spiritual growth. Just as the body needs material nutrition, the soul needs spiritual sustenance, which comes through communion with God. Our hearts are mirrors, so we need to focus these on the sun. Otherwise, the mirror benefits nothing in the dark. Our inner selves are like plants. If a plant remain in the shade and away from the light, its growth will be utterly impossible. However, if we move the plant into sunlight, it will grow and prosper. Therefore, we must make prayer our daily habit and try to pray every morning and evening.

As St. Thomas Aquinas has written: "The very giving ourselves to prayer has the effect of soothing our minds and purifying them; it makes us more fit to receive the Divine gifts which are spiritually poured out upon us."[95] When we are in a receptive mood, and supplicate God at morning and evening, we enable ourselves to become channels for God's grace and power, which flow through us like water through a canal. God is always dispensing His Light and power; it is up to us to be willing to receive it. "He is always ready," Aquinas says, "indeed, to give us His light, not, indeed, His visible light, but the light of the intellect and the spirit."[96] In order to give enough time to feed our souls with God's light, we should dedicate a fixed amount of time, say, at least five minutes every morning and evening. We can take advantage of the reverential and calm attitude we obtain through prayer to meditate before or after the prayer. On certain days, such as holy days, we can dedicate even more time to prayer and meditation. In short:

- We should remember that prayer is essential for spiritual growth
- We should pray every morning and evening, in order to grow closer to our Creator

- We should dedicate at least 5 minutes for each prayer
- We can take time to meditate before or after each prayer
- On holy days, we can dedicate more time to prayer and meditation

"Let not mercy and truth forsake thee: bind them about thy neck; write them upon the table of thine heart."[97]

- Proverbs 3:3

STEP 8 – LIVING IN A STATE OF PRAYER

Prayer should not simply be an activity in which we set aside a particular time and perform it. That is necessary, of course, but, even more importantly, we need to live lives which are in accordance with the Divine Will. When we live in a state of prayer, we put all our trust and faith in the Creative Force which gave us being. If God has brought us into being and continuously creates and sustains the entire universe, should we not have faith in God that He will provide for us? Therefore, we must constantly live in a state of supplication. When we need anything, we should internally turn to God for help. We should always remember God's grace and bounty and be thankful for what He has provided us with. As St. Augustine declared in his *Confessions*: "Thanks be to Thee, my Sweetness, my Honour and my Trust, O my God! Thanks be to Thee for Thy gifts! But do Thou keep them for me! For so doing Thou wilt be keeping me, and those things which Thou hast given me will be increased and perfected, and I myself shall be with Thee, for even that I should be at all is Thy gift to me!"[98]

> **"O Lord, O Ancient of days, Thy mercies, Whether known to us or unknown, are all from Thee!**
> **Thou hast commanded, saying, 'Remember thy God,'**
> **Because God's claims are never exhausted!"[99]**

- Jalālu'd-Dīn Rūmī, *The Masnavi*, Book III, Story II.

We should imagine that God is ever-present, being closer to us that our own veins and flesh. If we try to approach God through our thoughts and internal prayers, and remember Him throughout the day, then He will be near to us in spirit. As God—glorified be He—says in the Qur'ān: "And when my servants ask thee concerning me, then will I be nigh unto them. I will answer the cry of him that crieth, when he crieth unto me: but let them hearken unto me, and believe in me, that they may proceed aright."[100] The remembrance of God should be our constant companion. One way of achieving this is to wear some reminder of God's grace and help, such as a ring, pendant, t-shirt or arm-band. These could be engraved or covered in a message, a quotation or phrase which will help us to focus on our objective—that of God-consciousness and awareness of our purpose in life, i.e. to know and connect with the Divine Being, and to be filled with love and divine attributes. Some possible suggestions include: "Blessed be the name of thy Lord, full of majesty and glory,"[101] "And make mention of the name of thy Lord",[102] "And put thy trust in God,"[103] "God knoweth and beholdeth his servants,"[104] "Trust in the LORD with all thine heart,"[105] "The LORD is my light,"[106] "Love is the seed of happiness,"[107] "Happiness is the outcome of good,"[108] "Let not mercy and truth forsake thee,"[109] "Follow the law of virtue,"[110] "The superior man has neither anxiety nor fear,"[111] "Do all thou dost for Me!",[112] "In faith of Me all dangers thou shalt vanquish, by My grace,"[113] and "Retire into thyself."[114]

In addition, we can try to remind ourselves of God's presence by referring to the quotations from this book, or we can have a book of verses handy, so that we can refresh our memory while at the workplace or at home. If we own a Bible, or Qur'ān, Bhagavad-Gita or Dhammapada, or other book of scripture, we can keep this in sight, either on a table, bookshelf or desk, so that we are reminded of the Divine. We can also use a notebook of our own, in which we can write poignant quotations from the great religious teachers and philosophers of the past, or our own reflections on the spiritual life, and refer to this book from time to time during the course of the day, in order to remind ourselves of our life's purpose and the spiritual nature of man. In summary:

- We should remember to live our lives in accordance with the Divine Will
- We should live in a constant state of supplication to God

- We should always remember God's grace and bounty and be thankful for everything we have received
- We can remind ourselves of our life's purpose by wearing a ring, pendant, t-shirt or arm-band with a relevant phrase or quotation
- We can refer to quotations in this book in order to remember God
- We can keep a holy book in sight to remind ourselves of God and our purpose
- We can keep our own notebook and refer to it throughout the day

Questions for Reflection:

The following are some questions that will help us to reflect on what we have learned so far in this chapter:

1. What is the purpose of cleanliness and purity in relation to prayer?
2. How should we prepare ourselves to pray?
3. How can we praise God?
4. What should we ask God for?

5. How often should we pray and what does it mean to live in a state of prayer? How can we achieve such a state of being?

In the next chapter, we will look at the Third Way to Be—Magnanimity.

∞∞∞∞∞∞∞∞∞∞∞∞∞∞∞∞∞∞∞∞∞∞∞∞∞∞

VII. THIRD WAY TO BE – MAGNANIMITY

Parable:

"A prince inherited immense riches by succeeding to his father. He opened the hand of liberality, displayed his munificence, and bestowed innumerable gifts upon his troops and people... A narrow-minded courtier began to admonish him, saying, 'Verily, former sovereigns have collected this wealth with scrupulosity and stored it advisedly. Check your hand in this waste, for accidents wait ahead, and foes lurk behind. God forbid that you should want it on a day of need.— Wert thou to distribute the contents of a granary among the people, every master of a family might receive a grain of rice; why not exact a grain of silver from each, that thou mightest daily hoard a chamber full of treasure?'

"The prince turned his face aside from this speech, so contrary to his own lofty sentiments, and harshly reprimanded him, saying, 'A great and glorious God made me sovereign of this property, that I might enjoy and spend it; and posted me not a sentinel, to hoard and watch over it.— Carown[115] perished, who possessed forty magazines of treasure; Nushirowan[116] died

not, who left behind him a fair reputation.'"[117]

Saadi, *The Gulistan*, CH I, XVIII

Reflections:

In this parable, a prince or ruler has inherited the kingdom of his father. Instead of hoarding wealth and using it to fund his own opulence and grandeur, the prince decides to generously bestow his wealth on those in need, including his troops, who risk their lives on a daily basis to preserve his realm, and his people. One of his courtiers, who had a materialistic view of life, berates him for wasting the wealth that his father had accumulated. Instead, he argues that the prince should tax his people so that he can acquire a 'grain of silver from each'. The prince responds by arguing that God has conferred the wealth on him as a trustee, who should distribute it and use it for good. He gives the example of Qārūn, who grew haughty because of his wealth and was swallowed up into the earth. Likewise, he gives the contrasting example of the Persian king, Anushiruwān, who was noted for his wisdom and generosity. Even though this king lived in the sixth century CE, his reputation as 'the Just' has survived throughout the ages. The same may be said of Emperor Marcus Aurelius, who ruled Rome in the 2nd century CE. Being a practitioner of Stoicism who wrote about how to achieve equanimity in life, we have quoted him several times already throughout this book. He was yet another example of a king whose reputation for goodness has survived. Kings who hoard wealth are generally remembered as cruel and unjust.

> **"Acquire the contemplative way of seeing how all things change into one another, and constantly attend to it... for nothing is so much adapted to produce magnanimity... But as to what any man shall say or think about him or do against him, he never even thinks of it, being himself contented with these two things, with acting justly in what he now does, and being satisfied with what is now assigned to him... and desires nothing else than to accomplish the straight course through the law, and by accomplishing the straight course to follow God."**

- Marcus Aurelius, *Meditations*, Book X

Life is about sharing. We are not here on earth just to live our own individual lives, focused inwardly on our own needs and concerns. Rather, our very existence depends on cooperation. Civilization is based on cooperation. Society is based on cooperation. From the most basic utilities which we can all access, to the most basic questions of access to food, clean water and shelter, we are entirely dependent on our fellow human beings. Life is meant to be shared. If we want to be truly happy, we need to embrace our fellow human beings as travellers along the path to Truth. We must respect and love each and every person in our lives and recognize the higher self, the inner being, the soul within each one. It is often difficult to love those who cause us harm, or who are irritating or annoying. Nevertheless, by unleashing the power of **magnanimity**, by acknowledging the good and nobility within each human being, we can overcome hatred and animosity with the power of love.

What is magnanimity? It is not a common word in modern-day parlance, which is unfortunate. If this book can contribute to a wider currency for the word, that would be great, because magnanimity is the essence of true nobility. To be magnanimous is to be generous, forgiving, charitable and philanthropic towards others. To be magnanimous is to look an enemy in the face and turn the other cheek. To be magnanimous is to be bountiful, chivalrous and munificent. It means being high-minded towards one's rivals and willing to practise kindness to those who vie against us. It means being generous with our wealth and time, helping others when we can and giving of the excess of our prosperity. It means helping the poor and indigent, educating the ignorant, and providing for those in need. It means, in short, to treat others as we would like to be treated ourselves. Confucius said: "If you are generous, you will win all."[118] Generosity is the essence of true prosperity.

Jesus Christ gave the following parable to illustrate the futility of storing wealth and the inevitability that all things will pass away from us:

"And he said unto them, Take heed, and beware of covetousness: for a man's life consisteth not in the abundance of the things which he possesseth.

"And he spake a parable unto them, saying, The ground of a certain rich man

brought forth plentifully: And he thought within himself, saying, What shall I do, because I have no room where to bestow my fruits? And he said, This will I do: I will pull down my barns, and build greater; and there will I bestow all my fruits and my goods. And I will say to my soul, Soul, thou hast much goods laid up for many years; take thine ease, eat, drink, and be merry.

"But God said unto him, Thou fool, this night thy soul shall be required of thee: then whose shall those things be, which thou hast provided? So is he that layeth up treasure for himself, and is not rich toward God."[119]

- Luke 12:15 – 21

The moral of this story is: the man thought he could remain at ease and happy throughout his life, because he had stored up a great quantity of wealth in his many storehouses. By so doing, he hoped to spend the rest of his life in ease, eating, drinking and being merry. Nevertheless, that very night that he made the remark, hoping to life a long life of luxury, God took away his life and his pleasures were ended. Since he was not 'rich in God', and had spent his life and energies in accumulating wealth, his true purpose in life was not achieved and, at the moment of death, he experienced true loss.

True loss is to not know one's purpose in life and to live a fruitless life on earth. We can be incredibly successful and wealthy and live in the largest mansion and enjoy the greatest pleasures, but what will this avail us at the moment of death? We can conquer many nations and become master of all the world, as Alexander the Great did, or Napoleon Bonaparte, but what did they possess at the moment of death? How long did their empires even endure beyond their deaths? Their victories were fruitless and their achievements were meaningless, because they focused only on the material aspect of life and tried to accumulate wealth, power and sovereignty for themselves, instead of living a magnanimous life.

"O soul! whoever spreadeth the table of benevolence

Is famous in the world of liberality.

Generosity will make thee renowned throughout the universe;

Generosity will secure thee happiness."[120]

- Saadi, *Scroll of Wisdom*, In Praise of Generosity

Being magnanimous means giving away our time and money to others, and using them wisely ourselves. It does not mean becoming a recluse or only spending money on charity. Rather, it means living within one's means and saving for the future, while also giving generously to charities, helping others in need and helping our families. It also means giving time to others through volunteer work, educating others and spending quality time with our children and families. It means taking time to share knowledge with others, taking time to pray with others, taking time to listen to others, taking time to *be* with others. Furthermore, being magnanimous means living a life of high-mindedness, not looking at the faults of others, overlooking their shortcomings, remembering their inner nobility, and loving them as a brother loves a brother, a sister loves a sister, and as a father or mother loves their child. As St. Paul has written: "We then that are strong ought to bear the infirmities of the weak, and not to please ourselves. Let every one of us please his neighbour for his good to edification."[121]

Furthermore, Jesus Christ was asked, "Teacher, what must I do to inherit eternal life?"[122] Instead of answering, Jesus asked: "What is written in the law? How readest thou?"[123] The man replied, quoting from the Torah: "Thou shalt love the Lord thy God with all thy heart, and with all thy soul, and with all thy strength, and with all thy mind; and thy neighbour as thyself."[124] Jesus answered: "Thou hast answered right: this do, and thou shalt live."[125] Likewise, in the Qur'ān, God says—glorified be His glory: "They will ask thee what they shall bestow in alms. SAY: Let the good which ye bestow be for parents, and kindred, and orphans, and the poor, and the wayfarer; and whatever good ye do, of a truth God knoweth."[126] Just as God is generous to us, we should be generous to others, as He says: "See they not that God bestoweth full supplies on whom He pleaseth and giveth sparingly to whom He pleaseth? Signs truly are there herein to those who believe. To him who is of kin to thee give his due, and to the poor and to the wayfarer: this will be best for those who seek the face of God; and with them it shall be well."[127]

"Let us speak of beneficence and liberality, than which, indeed, nothing is more in harmony with human nature."[128]

- Cicero, *De Oficiis*, Book 1.14.

In short, magnanimity is the path to the good-pleasure to God. We should give our time and money to others with wisdom and should not amass great amounts of wealth for our sole enjoyment. We should give to our families, as well as to the poor and wayfarers—i.e. travellers. We should be kind and considerate to others and tolerant of those who disagree with us or do us harm. We should be forgiving and overlook the faults of others, and we should try to take the high road in every conflict. To be truly magnanimous, we should look to our inner nobility and the nobility of others, and remember that our lives are short. As Aristotle has written: "But virtuous acts, we said, are noble, and are done for the sake of that which is noble. The liberal man, therefore, like the others, will give with a view to, or for the sake of, that which is noble, and give rightly; i.e. he will give the right things to the right persons at the right times—in short, his giving will have all the characteristics of right giving."[129]

Questions for Reflection:

The following are some questions that will help us to reflect on what we have learned so far in this chapter:

1. What is magnanimity?
2. What are some ways to be magnanimous?
3. What is the moral of Saadi's story of the prince from the *Gulistān*?
4. Who should we be generous to?
5. What are some ways to be generous with our time?

In the next chapter, we will look at how to practise magnanimity.

∞∞∞∞∞∞∞∞∞∞∞∞∞∞∞∞∞∞∞∞∞∞∞∞∞

VIII. THE THIRD PRACTICE –
GENEROUS GIVING

"He that cleaves to wealth had better cast it away than allow his heart to be poisoned by it; but he who does not cleave to wealth, and possessing riches, uses them rightly, will be a blessing unto his fellows. It is not life and wealth and power that enslave men, but the cleaving to life and wealth and power."[130]

- Buddha, *The Gospel of Buddha*, p. 74

There are two main ways to be magnanimous. One, the most obvious, is to share our wealth with others. Sharing is not something that only wealthy people can do. And I am not advocating giving to beggars or wasting our money by throwing it up in the air in a public square or football stadium. Rather, I am advocating giving money wisely and compassionately. First of all, we should set aside a certain amount of money to give to charity, so that we can help others in need. This could be a small amount each month and we will discuss this further in the next chapter. If we are religious, we can also give away a certain percentage to our church, mosque, temple or religious charity. Next, we should put away some money for savings. Far from hoarding money, putting aside a certain amount for emergencies and for retirement is a responsible way to be generous to ourselves and our families in the future. Then, we should spend a certain amount of money on our family and loved ones, as well as on our expenses. Lastly, some money we could also use on entertainment or for personal purchases, e.g. buying a new book or watching a film. We should not live lives of austerity, but should, rather, take advantage of healthy pursuits, pastimes, holidays and enjoyment, without being frivolous or wasteful.

"Every man according as he purposeth in his heart, so let him give; not grudgingly, or of necessity: for God loveth a cheerful giver."[131]

- 2 Corinthians 9:7

The other way to be magnanimous is through giving our time to others. When we agree to help someone out, when we volunteer for a charity, when we educate someone, when we give our time to listen to and enjoy the company of others, we are being generous. We should always be willing to consider the needs of others, both physically and emotionally. This is especially applicable when it comes to family members, who need our time more than others. When our hearts are filled with love, there is always time to give. When we love our children, there is always time to provide for their moral education. After our own parents, spouse and children, next in our responsibility comes those who live around us—our neighbours. We should be willing to help them when they are in need, give them food when they are hungry, lend them things when they need them. But, most of all, we should listen to and respect them, and provide them with the seeds of guidance. If we are aware of any truth, or any wisdom, we should share it with others, especially those nearest and dearest to us.

"But whoso hath this world's good, and seeth his brother have need, and shutteth up his bowels of compassion from him, how dwelleth the love of God in him?"[132]

- 1 John 3:17

After the neighbourhood, our responsibility extends to our local community (village, town or borough), where there are always many opportunities to give one's time to helping others. This could be through community education activities, through charitable events, or through setting up moral classes for children and youth. Another good way to help others is to set up groups to learn about the development of virtues and morality, or prayer circles where people of all different faiths and backgrounds get together to read quotations from sacred writings and pray to the one Creative Force which brought us all into existence. After the local community, our responsibility extends to the nation, and then to all mankind.

We should always think of the interests of the whole above those of the local and individual. If we give money to a charity to support refugees, we are helping our fellow brothers and sisters who live in other parts of the world. All of us were created by one God and are the children of one family. We are as much responsible for our brothers in Honduras or Cameroon, in China or India, as we are for people within our own countries, because God has given us a responsibility to love one another and care for one another. If there are children—or adults—going hungry in any part of the world, that means we, as the human race, are not living up to our collective responsibility. The problems of other nations are not *their* problems—they are *our* problems.

> **"O ye folk! fear your Lord, who created you from one soul, and created therefrom its mate, and diffused from them twain many men and women."[133]**
>
> - Qur'ān 4:1

Indeed, we can only really acquire true magnanimity when we realize that the whole of humanity is one organic whole. In the Qur'ān, God says—exalted be He: "O men! verily, we have created you of a male and a female; and we have divided you into peoples and tribes that ye might have knowledge one of another. Truly, the most worthy of honour in the sight of God is he who feareth Him most. Verily, God is Knowing, Cognisant,"[134] and He says: "Mankind was but one people; and God sent prophets to announce glad tidings and to warn."[135] On our duty to others, He likewise says: "Be good to parents, and to kindred, and to orphans, and to the poor, and to a neighbour, whether kinsman or new-comer, and to a fellow traveller, and to the wayfarer."[136] The same sentiment is echoed in the New Testament, where St. Paul says: "There is neither Jew nor Greek, there is neither bond nor free, there is neither male nor female: for ye are all one in Christ Jesus."[137] And in the Gospel of John, Jesus Christ commands his followers: "A new commandment I give unto you, That ye love one another; as I have loved you, that ye also love one another. By this shall all men know that ye are my disciples, if ye have love one to another."[138]

In the next chapter, we will give some practical steps for practising magnanimity in our daily lives.

Questions for Reflection:

The following are some questions that will help us to reflect on what we have learned so far in this chapter:

1. What are the different things that we should spend money on?
2. What is the other way to be magnanimous?

3. How can we be responsible for our neighbourhoods?
4. After our neighbourhoods, what are we responsible for?
5. What is our responsibility to humankind? How should we regard humanity?

∞∞∞∞∞∞∞∞∞∞∞∞∞∞∞∞∞∞∞∞∞∞∞∞

IX. GENEROUS GIVING – STEPS FOR FURTHER DEVELOPMENT

To achieve magnanimity, we must be generous. The following are five steps to practise generosity and develop the art of magnanimity.

> **"Give, and it shall be given unto you; good measure, pressed down, and shaken together, and running over, shall men give into your bosom. For with the same measure that ye mete withal it shall be measured to you again."**[139]

\- Luke 6:38

FIRST STEP – SET ASIDE MONEY FOR CHARITY

This step is simplicity itself. Whatever we earn, we should set aside a certain amount for charity, so that we can help others who are in need. Charity is the essence of kindness, because it is sharing of one's wealth with others. Even the poorest individual can give to others, whether it be a homeless man who shares a piece of bread with his companion, or a rich executive who shares millions of his wealth with the poor and needy. The act, in itself, is key. By being generous we are not only helping to make the world a better place, we are also purifying ourselves and our intentions and bringing ourselves more in line with the Divine Will which created us. As God is the Most Magnanimous and the All-Generous, so likewise we must reflect and mirror this attribute in every aspect of our lives.

The easiest way to do this is to set a fixed amount to give to a fixed number of charities. In most cases, one would only select one charity or charitable organization to give to. But those who have greater means may choose to give to more. As such, I have compiled a list of recommended charities and non-profit organizations which can be found on my blog, here: https://fivewaystobe.wordpress.com/2017/02/06/recommended-charities-charitable-organizations/. How much one chooses to donate to any particular charity is a matter for the individual to decide based on their means. I would suggest either a fixed percentage, such as 2% or 5% annually, or a fixed amount, such as $20, $50, $100, $250, or $500 per month.

"If a brother or sister be naked, and destitute of daily food, and one of you say unto them, Depart in peace, be ye warmed and filled; notwithstanding ye give them not those things which are needful to the body; what doth it profit?"[140]

- James 2:15 – 16

As I mentioned in the preface to this book, my wife and I have founded a charitable organization called **Msingi wa Tumaini**, which means 'Foundation of Hope' in Swahili. Msingi wa Tumaini is endeavouring to change the lives of children in rural Kenya, particularly in the village of Uyoma, which lies in western Kenya, on the shores of Lake Victoria. When we visited the area more than five years ago and saw the poverty and suffering of many of the children there, we knew we had to do something to help. My wife suggested that we start a charity, which would help children gain access to education. In particular, we focused our attention on the numerous orphans and other vulnerable children in the area. Many of these were orphaned due to HIV and are being raised by their grandparents or other relatives. Many do not have shoes, and all of them have to walk to the local school, Gagra Primary School, which was built by my father-in-law many decades ago.

By providing school lunches for children at the school, we have tried to increase access to education, as children are unable to go home during the day for food. We have also distributed sanitary towels for girls, as this is another typical barrier to education, increasing the number of girls who are able to attend the school. For more information, please visit http://mwtumaini.org/ or follow us on Twitter: https://twitter.com/mwtumaini and Facebook: https://www.facebook.com/Msingi-wa-Tumaini-274916052612441/?fref=ts. You can also donate to Msingi wa Tumaini via JustGiving.

Regular, monthly donations would greatly assist Msingi wa Tumaini to achieve its objectives. YOU can help to make our projects successful by donating NOW or by setting up a regular, monthly donation.

If you are a member of a church, mosque, temple or other religious organization, it would also be a good idea to give a certain fixed amount to your faith group.

In addition, one can give to local charities. I am sure there is a local charity in your area which needs support. Sometimes, we may not even be aware of local opportunities to help and share our wealth with those who are closest to us. In short:

- Giving is the key to developing magnanimity, as it is an attribute of the Divine Being
- We should give a fixed amount to a charity, such as an annual percentage or a monthly fixed amount
- The author recommends giving a fixed, monthly donation to Msingi wa Tumaini, which helps orphans and vulnerable children in rural Kenya
- We should also give donations to our church, mosque, temple or faith organization
- We can also give to local charities, which help to support our local communities

∞∞∞∞∞∞∞∞∞∞∞∞∞∞∞∞∞∞∞∞∞∞∞∞∞∞∞

"There is that scattereth, and yet increaseth; and there is that withholdeth more than is meet, but it tendeth to poverty. The liberal soul shall be made fat: and he that watereth shall be watered also himself."[141]

- Proverbs 11:24 – 25

SECOND STEP – SAVE FOR YOUR FUTURE

While we should give to others, we should also be responsible in how we spend and save our money. There is a big difference between hoarding wealth and saving and investing responsibly. As we give, so do we increase. He who strives, succeeds. And he who gives, receives. This is a natural law of the universe. When we give to others, God increases what we have. And of this increase, we should put aside a fixed amount or percentage each month to save for our future. It could be a sort of retirement fund or other savings fund which will allow us to live comfortably in old age and help us to provide for our children. It will also allow us to invest in a business, if we wish, or give even more to charity, if we so choose. In short:

- Invest in yourself by setting aside a fixed amount for savings every month
- This money can be used for your retirement or future investment

"Verily, God enjoineth justice and the doing of good and gifts to kindred, and he forbiddeth wickedness and wrong and oppression. He warneth you that haply ye may be mindful."[142]

- Qur'ān 16:90

"Moreover we have enjoined on man to shew kindness to parents."[143]

- Qur'ān 29:8

THIRD STEP – SUPPORT YOUR FAMILY

When we have thus set aside excess income towards charity and our savings, we should use our income to support our families. This means supporting ourselves, our wives or husbands, and our children. It may even extend further, in some cases, with grandparents providing financial support to their grandchildren, especially in difficult economic times.

Likewise, in many societies, when parents get older, there is no government-mandated social support system. In such cases, children should also use money to provide for their parents. Ordinarily, the burden of responsibility for one's parents would fall on the eldest child, or children. In any case, as we read in the Qur'ān above, giving to one's kindred is an act of virtue, and showing kindness to one's parents is a responsibility ordained by the Creator. We should also take time to listen to our family members and spend quality time with them, showing love and companionship. This is also a charitable act and a sign of generosity. Let us remember:

- We should spend money to support our families
- We should, in some cases, also support our parents financially
- We should show kindness to our parents
- We should spend quality time with our family members

"Generosity is to do a kindness before it is asked, and to pity and give a man who asks."[144]

- An Arabian proverb

FOURTH STEP – HELP YOUR NEIGHBOURHOOD AND COMMUNITY

After our own families, we should extend support to our communities. Though we mentioned local charities above, this usually takes the form of giving time and energy, rather than financial support. We can help to start a children's moral education class or moral development programme for young people. We can also start a prayer circle or group to share spiritual quotations and prayers. We can take part in local community development projects and other artistic, educational and musical activities. The needs of every community differ greatly and the needs and activities of a small village in Wales will differ greatly from those of a rural village in India or Bangladesh. It is very difficult, therefore, to come up with any hard and fast rules in relations to this point. In short:

- We can give our time to our local communities through volunteer work
- We can start a children's moral education class or youth moral development class
- We can start a prayer group to share quotations and prayers
- We can take part in and support local development projects
- We can take part in and support local artistic, educational and musical activities

"Be generous to the extent of thy power. If thou hast not dug a well in the desert, at least place a lamp in a shrine."[145]

- Saadi, *The Bustan*, Chapter II.

FIFTH STEP – FIND A CAUSE TO SUPPORT

We each have our own passions and issues which really move us, at the core of our being. Some people, like myself, are passionate about children's education. Others are passionate about women's rights, preventing female genital mutilation or providing relief for refugees. Whatever the cause, we should find a focus—a problem that we can contribute to solving, even if only financially. If we are able, we can even get involved directly, through volunteering for a charity or non-profit organization. We can focus locally or internationally. Whatever the case, I recommend that you think about what really moves you and try to take an initiative to try and solve that problem. You may even have the means and desire to found your own charity or voluntary organization. In short:

- Find what really moves you and focus on trying to solve the problem, even if only financially
- Volunteer your time where possible
- You may even wish to found your own charity or voluntary organization, if you are able

Questions for Reflection:

The following are some questions that will help us to reflect on what we have learned in this chapter:

1. How should we go about setting aside money for charity? What organizations should we give money to?
2. Why should we save for our future? And how should we go about it?
3. How should we support our families?

4. What are some ways we can help our neighbourhoods and local communities?
5. How should we act once we have found a cause we support?
6. In the next chapter, we will look at the Fourth Way to Be—Contemplation.

∞∞∞∞∞∞∞∞∞∞∞∞∞∞∞∞∞∞∞∞∞∞∞∞∞∞

X. FOURTH WAY TO BE – CONTEMPLATION

Parable:

"And the Blessed One thus addressed the brethren:

'Those only who do not believe, call me Gotama, but you call me the Buddha, the Blessed One, the Teacher. And this is right, for I have in this life entered Nirvāna, while the life of Gotama has been extinguished...

'I myself having reached the other shore, help others to cross the stream; I myself having attained salvation, am a saviour of others; being comforted, I comfort others and lead them to the place of refuge...

'The subject on which I meditate is truth. The practice to which I devote myself is truth. The topic of my conversation is truth. My thoughts are always in the truth. For lo! my self has become the truth.

'Whosoever comprehendeth the truth will see the Blessed One, for the truth has been preached by the Blessed One.'"[146]

- Buddha, *The Gospel of Buddha*, LIV., pp. 160 – 163.

Reflections:

In this account from the life of Gautama Buddha, he explains the essence of his creed, which is that life and all that is in the physical world, is impermanent. The body of Gautama has turned to dust and is no more. No one alive today may see the face of the Buddha, listen to his voice or enter his physical presence. He has moved on to a realm which is beyond materiality—he has entered the realm of the All-Highest Paradise, which Buddhism refers to as the state of Nirvāna. Nirvāna means the extinction of ego. It is often interpreted as meaning the extinction of one's self, i.e. one's soul or essence. However, this is not the real meaning. To extinguish oneself means to extinguish one's ego, the lower self, the animal self which prompts us to serve our own interests to the exclusion of others. In reality, we can only acquire virtues by extinguishing the flames of this lower self and awakening the higher susceptibilities of the soul, which is our higher self. Being completely liberated from self and passion, Gautama Buddha had attained to the state of Nirvāna, even though he was still alive at the time. Nirvāna does not depend on life or death—it is a condition of self-abnegation and self-realization, which we may call **detachment**—the **First Way to Be** described in this book.

In the context of this talk, Buddha refers to himself as if he were an ordinary human being, who has achieved Nirvāna through his own efforts. When we look at other references to himself, however, we realise that he was, actually, a higher being, a pure Manifestation of the Divine—who, like a pure mirror, reflects and manifests all of the divine attributes in his person. Thus did he say above, "but you call me the Buddha, the Blessed One, the Teacher."[147] Elsewhere, he refers to himself as the Tathagāta, which means 'one who has thus arrived'.[148] In Chapter XIV of the Dhammapada, he says: "A supernatural person (a Buddha) is not easily found, he is not born everywhere. Wherever such a sage is born, that race prospers. Happy is the arising of the awakened, happy is the teaching of the True Law, happy is peace in the church, happy is the devotion of those who are at peace."[149] In order to truly achieve Nirvāna, and fully realize our purpose in life, we have to turn to such a True Guide, such a Tathāgata, Teacher or Blessed One, and accept his teachings. As they are pure and abundant conduits of the Divine, we can experience divine blessings and abundant spiritual growth by turning to these Great Teachers.

> **"He who takes refuge with the Buddha, the Law, and the Church; he who, with clear understanding, sees the four holy truths:— viz. pain, the origin of pain, the destruction of pain, and the eightfold holy way that leads to the quieting of pain;— That is the safe refuge, that is the best refuge; having gone to that refuge, a man is delivered from all pain."[150]**
>
> - Buddha, *The Dhammapada*, Ch. XIV, v. 190 – 192

In the quotation above, 'the Law' is an interpretation of the word Dharma, which is the eternal Way of Truth, the teachings of the Great Teachers. The Church means the community of the followers of the Buddha. But this quotation does not apply to Buddha alone. It applies, also, to all those Great Teachers who have appeared in the world, such as Krishna, Abraham, Zoroaster, Moses, Jesus Christ and Muhammad, may the peace and blessings of God be upon all of them. By turning to these Great Teachers, we are seeking refuge with our Creator and accepting His Will for the world, which is the essence of detachment and renunciation. This is the essence of submission to the Divine Will, which allows us to rely on God alone. By submitting ourselves to God, we are conditioning ourselves with pure intent and sincerity. This is also a precondition for true prayer and supplication to the Divine.

"In the adorations and benedictions of righteous men

The praises of all the prophets are kneaded together.

All their praises are mingled into one stream,

All the vessels are emptied into one ewer.

Because He that is praised is, in fact, only One.

In this respect all religions are only one religion.

Because all praises are directed towards God's Light,

These various forms and figures are borrowed from it."[151]

- Rūmī, *The Masnavī*

A word on the subject of religious and philosophical differences: if we recognize the Truth, we should accept it in whatever form and place it may be. If we are lovers of the Light, we do not care in what Lamp it may appear. If we are lovers of the sun, we do not care if it arises yesterday or tomorrow—we love the sun regardless.

So, if we accept the Light contained within the inner essence of one of these Great Teachers, we need to recognize the Light contained within each and ALL of them. We cannot deny the Light, as the Light is ONE.

We cannot deny the Dharma—the Way of the Truth—whether it be taught by one Teacher or another. They all teach the same Dharma—the same religion, the same philosophy, the same way of life. Contradictions only exist on the level of materiality and limited human conceptions and dogmas, but not on the level of reality. Therefore, before we enter upon the path of true contemplation—true meditation—we should take refuge with the Buddha, and all the Great Teachers, and accept their Teachings. This will set us upon the Path of Truth—the Middle Way—the Straight Path.

In the fourth paragraph of the story cited above, Buddha states what the subject of *his* meditation is— which is Truth. In other words, meditation is not just about controlling breathing, posture, seating positions, etc. and clearing the mind. Those are all important things for focused meditation, of course, but the essence of meditation is contemplation on the matter of Truth. One way of doing that is contemplating the reality of existence, and the signs of Truth which appear before us.

Contemplation and reflection is constantly mentioned in the Qur'ān, where God says—praised be He: "On Earth are signs for men of firm belief, and also in your own selves: Will ye not then behold them? The Heaven hath sustenance for you, and it containeth that which you are promised. By the Lord then of the heaven and of the earth, I swear that this is the truth, even as ye speak yourselves."[152] If you want to meditate on the essence of Truth, I recommend that you read through the Qur'ān, which is full of topics for contemplation—all of which lead back to the central essence of Truth, which is the knowledge of God. The

Qur'ān is full of parables, mostly Biblically-based, which each have deep moral teachings and hidden wisdom. As He says: "And now have we set before men, in this Koran, every kind of parable."[153]

In one parable, for example, the Qur'ān gives the example of two gardens—vineyards—surrounded by palm trees, with corn fields between them. Each of the two gardens yielded fruit and benefits for their owners. In addition, in the midst of the gardens, there was a river. Consumed with material desires, the owner of one of the gardens said to the other: "More have I than thou of wealth, and my family is mightier."[154] Then, when he returned to his garden, he said: "I do not think that this will ever perish: And I do not think that 'the Hour' will come: and even if I be taken back to my Lord, I shall surely find a better than it in exchange."[155]

The other gardener rebuked him, saying: "What! hast thou no belief in him who created thee of the dust, then of the germs of life, then fashioned thee a perfect man? But God is my Lord; and no other being will I associate with my Lord. And why didst thou not say when thou enteredst thy garden, 'What God willeth! There is no power but in God.' Though thou seest that I have less than thou of wealth and children, yet haply my Lord may bestow on me better than thy garden, and may send his bolts upon it out of Heaven, so that the next dawn shall find it barren dust; or its water become deep sunk, so that thou art unable to find it."[156]

Even as the second gardener had predicted, the first gardener's vines were destroyed, falling from their trellises, and his fruits were last. He had neither the means to help himself nor his garden. This is, the Qur'ān informs us, a similitude of life itself.[157] We become attached to the material world and forget that nothing really lasts. There is nothing material which we should set our hearts upon. There is nothing which we can really regard as lasting and enduring. All things pass away. God says: "And set before them a similitude of the present life. It is as water which we send down from Heaven, and the herb of the Earth is mingled with it, and on the morrow it becometh dry stubble which the winds scatter: for God hath power over all things."[158] Our wealth and children, He says, "are the adornment of this present life". The adornment of spiritual reality, of the Kingdom of God, however, are good words, "which are lasting, are better in the sight of thy Lord as to recompense, and better as to hope."[159]

> **"Seest thou not to what God likeneth a good word? To a good tree: its root firmly fixed, and its branches in the Heaven: Yielding its fruit in all seasons by the will of its Lord. God setteth forth these similitudes to men that haply they may reflect."[160]**
>
> - Qur'ān 14:24 – 25

The essence of this parable is the same as the essence of Buddha's teaching, which is to be detached from the material world, to abandon the lower self— the ego—and to embrace the path of virtue. It is not possible to achieve this without reflection, without contemplation, without mindfulness. God has sent down the Qur'ān, He says, "that haply they may fear God, or that it may give birth to reflection in them."[161] Likewise, He says: "SAY: Will ye not, then reflect?",[162] "And he hath subjected to you all that is in the Heavens and all that is on the Earth: all is from him. Verily, herein are signs for those who reflect,"[163] and "Thus God maketh plain his signs to you that ye may reflect."[164] In fact, the entire Qur'ān is full of admonitions for man to reflect, to consider, to remember. If we are to attain to the Straight Path and follow it, then we must reflect—we must contemplate reality. We should consider nature, the world around us, the meaning of life, death, suffering, God and the Great Teachers who bring His Message.

"Look within. Within is the fountain of good, and it will ever bubble up, if thou wilt ever dig."[165]
- Marcus Aurelius, *Meditations*, Book VII

How, then, should we contemplate or meditate? We have already referred to this in the First Practice, which revolves around the Eightfold Path of the Buddha. Meditation can take many forms. In general, however, we should contemplate the Truth, which is the highest form of mindfulness. We should remember that we are only wayfarers in this world, destined to die and move on to another. We are only captains on a ship, and the ship will eventually reach its goal or founder, but in either case will return to the depths of the sea. Before we even set foot on the shores of the other world, we should divest ourselves of the ego—the lower self—which keeps us from reaching our goal. **We should die to ourselves and live in the love of God, which is the Fifth Way to Be.** We will discuss this later. For now, however, let us consider the topic of contemplation and meditation.

Questions for Reflection:

The following are some questions that will help us to reflect on what we have learned in this chapter:

1. What does Buddha meditate on?
2. What does Nirvāna ultimately mean?
3. What are the names of some of the Great Teachers? What is the effect of taking refuge in their Teachings?
4. Why should we be lovers of the Light, rather than the Lamp?
5. What is the meaning of the parable of the two gardens mentioned in the Qur'ān?

In the next chapter, we will look at some practical ways to practice contemplation.

∞∞∞∞∞∞∞∞∞∞∞∞∞∞∞∞∞∞∞∞∞∞∞∞∞∞

XI. THE FOURTH PRACTICE – MEDITATION

"O brethren, ye to whom the truth has been made known, having thoroughly made yourselves masters of it, practise it, meditate upon it, and spread it abroad, in order that pure religion may last long and be perpetuated, in order that it may continue for the good and happiness of the great multitudes, out of pity for the world, and to the good and gain of all living beings!"[166]

- Buddha, *The Gospel of Buddha*, XCIV, p. 236

We learned in the previous chapter that the true focus of meditation should be on Truth. Buddha said: "The subject on which I meditate is truth... Whosoever comprehendeth the truth will see the Blessed One, for the truth has been preached by the Blessed One."[167] In other words, if we meditate on the truth and understand the truth, then we will become aware of the Reality of the Buddha. As the Buddha is a pure conduit of the Divine, a Great Teacher imbued with spiritual power, this means that we will gain access to the highest level of knowledge—

Divine knowledge. Elsewhere, Buddha instructs us to "meditate on the Buddha and weigh his righteous law." He goes on to say: "We are encompassed on all sides by the rocks of birth, old age, disease, and death, and only by considering and practising the true law can we escape from this sorrow-piled mountain. What profit, then, in practising iniquity? All who are wise spurn the pleasures of the body. They loathe lust and seek to promote their spiritual existence."[168] He also states that we should "meditate deeply on the vanity of earthly things, and understand the fickleness of life."[169]

The topics of meditation are defined in some later Buddhist writings, such as the *Visuddhi-Magga*, which mentions 'forty subjects of meditation', including the 'ten reflections', which are topics of reflection. These include reflection on the Buddha, the Dharma, conduct and magnanimity, as well as contemplation of death, the body, breathing and quiescence.[170] In the *Samyutta-Nikâya*, the process of obtaining liberation from the material world and the ego is described in terms of four 'trances'. In each stage, one gradually transcends 'the voice', 'reasoning and reflection', 'joy' and 'the inspirations and expirations'. At such a stage, one enters 'the realm of the infinity of consciousness', etc. The goal is that all depravity, passion, hatred and infatuation should be completely extirpated from oneself.[171] I have not tried this method and would assume that one can learn more about this process from experienced Buddhist monks and practitioners.

"And is there anything more akin to wisdom than truth?"[172]

- Plato, *The Republic*, Book VI.

I would recommend that you start with something simpler than that which we have just mentioned. Follow Step 8 – Right Contemplation, which can be found in Chapter III. The points from Step 8 are repeated here for your convenience:

- In order to meditate, find a quiet and secluded place, or your bedroom
- Concentrate on your breathing, using deep breaths
- Focus your meditation on achieving a higher level of spiritual awareness

- Read verses aloud in order to focus on their sound and meaning

In particular, try to focus your meditation on attaining Truth. Resign yourself to the Higher Being which made you and ask to seek refuge in His Teachings and the Great Teachers whom He has sent to the world, such as Buddha and Christ. Remember that the Truth is one, but the Messengers are many. Remember that the Light is one, but the Lamps are many.

"Thou art hidden, yet revealest our hidden secrets.

Thou art the Source that causes our rivers to flow."[173]

- Rūmī, *The Masnavī*

Reflect upon the impermanence of life. As Buddha says above, we should "meditate deeply on the vanity of earthly things, and understand the fickleness of life." In *The Imitation of Christ*, Thomas à Kempis writes: "When it is morning reflect that it may be thou shalt not see the evening, and at eventide dare not to boast thyself of the morrow. Always be thou prepared, and so live that death may never find thee unprepared. Many die suddenly and unexpectedly... Who will remember thee after thy death? And who will entreat for thee? Work, work now, oh dearly beloved, work all that thou canst. For thou knowest not when thou shalt die, nor what shall happen unto thee after death. While thou hast time, lay up for thyself undying riches. Think of nought but of thy salvation; care only for the things of God. Make to thyself friends, by venerating the saints of God and walking in their steps, that when thou failest, thou mayest be received into everlasting habitations."[174]

If we remember that we are only wayfarers on earth, if we constantly meditate on the temporary nature of this physical life, then we can raise ourselves to a higher level of consciousness. Thomas à Kempis continues: "Keep thyself as a stranger and a pilgrim upon the earth, to whom the things of the world appertain not. Keep thine heart free, and lifted up towards God, for here have we no continuing city."[175]

Imagine a state—a condition in which we have a free heart, lifted up towards God! Imagine how wonderful it is to live without attachment, without being weighed down by the gnawing concerns, the perpetual burden of material attachment. What it means is freedom! What it means is being able to feel truly free from the cage of materialism. Here, we have no continuing city. By this, Thomas à Kempis means that we have no permanent lodging in this world. Here, we have no permanent abode. Rather, we are travellers passing through this life, helping others along the way, and passing on to a world to come. Now, I am alive. But tomorrow, I may not be. In a hundred years—or a thousand—you may still be reading this book, and I will be gone, abiding eternally in another realm. Reflect upon this! The same fate will befall you as well. So let us detach ourselves and meditate on what truly matters—the Truth.

"This, then, is consistent with the character of a reflecting man, to be neither careless nor impatient nor contemptuous with respect to death, but to wait for it as one of the operations of nature. As thou now waitest for the time when the child shall come out of thy wife's womb, so be ready for the time when thy soul shall fall out of this envelope."[176]

- Marcus Aurelius, *Meditations*, Book IX.

Thomas à Kempis, furthermore, gives specific recommendations for spiritual practice. He writes that we should "seek a suitable time" for meditation and "think frequently of the mercies of God." He continues: "If thou withdraw thyself from trifling conversation and idle goings about, as well as from novelties and gossip, thou shalt find thy time sufficient and apt for good meditation." When we feel ready to meditate, he says, we should enter our rooms and "shut out the tumults of the world." "Commune with your own heart in your own chamber and be still," he says. "In retirement thou shalt find what often thou wilt lose abroad. Retirement, if thou continue therein, groweth sweet, but if thou keep not in it, begetteth weariness. If in the beginning of thy conversation thou dwell in it and keep it well, it shall afterwards be to thee a dear friend, and a most pleasant solace. In silence and quiet the devout soul goeth forward and learneth the hidden things of the Scriptures. Therein findeth she a fountain of tears, wherein to wash and cleanse herself each night, that she may grow the more dear to her Maker as she dwelleth the further from all worldly distraction. To him who withdraweth himself from his acquaintance and friends God with his holy angels will draw nigh. It is better to be unknown and take heed to oneself than to neglect oneself and work wonders."[177]

The key points from the above quotations from Thomas à Kempis are:

- Imagine that you are a stranger or wayfarer on earth, just passing through to the next stage of your existence
- Avoid gossip, frivolity and idleness
- Withdraw to the seclusion of your room and "shut out the tumults of the world"
- Commune with your heart—your inner being—and sit still
- Remaining in silence is a habit which takes practice and cultivation
- In silent meditation, we can come to understand the mysteries of the Scriptures
- By withdrawing ourselves from the material realm, we become associated with the inhabitants of the spiritual realm above

These are just some recommendations, but you will find many more ways to meditate as you continue along the spiritual path. I hope to eventually release a book with more information on how to practise meditation. Please make sure to follow me @equanimityblog on Twitter so that you can get updates about any upcoming book releases. You can also follow my personal Twitter page @Nicholas19.

Some additional steps for further development will be given in the next chapter.

Questions for Reflection:

The following are some questions that will help us to reflect on what we have learned in this chapter:

1. What should we meditate on, according to Buddha?
2. What is the goal of meditation, according to some of the Buddhist scriptures mentioned above?
3. What should we remember when we meditate?
4. What are the points mentioned in Step 8 above?
5. What does Thomas à Kempis recommend? How does he say we should meditate?

∞∞∞∞∞∞∞∞∞∞∞∞∞∞∞∞∞∞∞∞∞∞∞∞

XI. MEDITATION – STEPS FOR FURTHER DEVELOPMENT

To practise true contemplation, we must use an effective method of meditation. The following are five steps to help us get the most from our meditation.

"The Spirit of God hath made me, and the breath of the Almighty hath given me life."[178]

- Job 33:4

FIRST STEP – MINDFULNESS OF BREATHING

In *The Religion of the Samurai*, Kaiten Nukariya writes: "The sole means of securing mental calmness is the practice of Zazen, or the sitting in Meditation..."[179] Zen is a type of Buddhism which has a strong focus on mental training and solving problems through meditation. Thus, they may ask themselves, 'What is Buddha?' and meditate on this problem. One Zen master, called Ten Shwai, used to put three questions to himself: Where does the real nature of the mind exist? How can you be saved when you are on the verge of death? and Where do you go when your body is reduced to the elements? Rather than theorizing or presenting arguments, Zen pupils take up the task of meditating on these problems in order to gain insights and revelations of truth.

The first step in the practice of Zen mental training is to become the master of external things. If we are addicted or attached to worldly pleasures, then we are the servants of external things. In describing such a 'servant', To Ju (Na-kae) says: "There is a great jail, not a jail for criminals, that contains the world in it. Fame, gain, pride, and bigotry form its four walls. Those who are confined in it fall a prey to sorrow and sigh for ever."[180] In order to achieve mastery over oneself, one must, according to Nukariya, "shut up all our senses, and turn the currents of thoughts inward, and see ourselves as the centre of the world, and meditate that we are the beings of highest intelligence; that Buddha never puts us at the mercy of natural forces; that the earth is in our possession; that everything on earth is to be made use of for our noble ends; that fire, water, air, grass, trees, rivers, hills, thunder, cloud, stars, the moon, the sun, are at our command; that we are the law-givers of the natural phenomena; that we are the makers of the phenomenal world; that it is we that appoint a mission through life, and determine the fate of man."[181]

This may seem to be an exalted position to put oneself in, but, in reality, it simply means becoming aware of our nature as mirrors of the Divine. As we are recipients of Divine guidance, so our heart is the mirror of all created things, and we are at the centre of all things. In Zen Buddhism, however, there is no specific mention of the 'Divine'. Instead, in order to achieve enlightenment, according to Nukariya, we "must establish the authority of Self over the whole body. We must use our bodies as we use our clothes in order to accomplish our noble purposes."[182] In this context, the self refers not to the lower self—the ego—but to the higher self, which is the soul. The first step is to sit in a quiet place and meditate, imagining that the body is no longer your bondage but, rather, that it is a machine which can work for your life. You are the governor of that body and can control it. It is something separate from your real self. If it disobeys you, correct it. If it is out-of-control, tame it. This requires a lot of practice. We should train our bodies to be able to endure any kind of suffering and be unflinching in the face of hardship.

First, seat yourself on a thick cushion. You should keep your body erect so that the tip of your nose and your navel are in one perpendicular line. Nukariya recommends that you put your right foot on your left thigh and the left foot on the right thigh—i.e. seat yourself cross-legged. This is not easy for everyone, but I am just outlining the typical Zen practice. Next, put your right hand, palm raised upwards, on the left foot and vice versa. Keep your eyes open during the whole meditation session. Do not breathe through the mouth. Instead, swell your abdomen as you breathe through your nose. Breathe in and out at regular intervals, holding each breath from one to ten. If you cannot do this, it is a sign that you are still distracted. Try to overcome this through regular practice. Controlling our breath allows us to control our minds. Focus on the spiritual questions mentioned above, or on the nature of suffering and impermanence. Try to master your body. In short:

- We should focus on answering questions, such as 'What is Buddha?' 'How can we achieve salvation from the material world?' and 'How does my soul transcend death?'

- We should recognize that the body is like a prison. We can be either the servant of the body or we can break free and become its master.
- The body is a machine. We can be the operators and controllers of that machine.
- We should see ourselves at the centre of all things, because we are mirrors of the Divine
- Sit in a quiet place on a thick cushion/mat, cross-legged with our palms facing upwards
- Keep your eyes open
- Keep your back straight and your nose and navel in line with one another
- Breathe through your nose, holding each breath as you count from one-to-ten
- Learn to transcend the body, and you will be able to endure any suffering and hardship

"The first meditation is the meditation of love in which thou must so adjust thy heart that thou longest for the weal and welfare of all beings, including the happiness of thine enemies. The second meditation is

the meditation of pity, in which thou thinkest of all beings in distress, vividly representing in thine imagination their sorrows and anxieties so as to arouse a deep compassion for them in thy soul. The third meditation is the meditation of joy in which thou thinkest of the prosperity of others and rejoicest with their rejoicings. The fourth meditation is the meditation on impurity, in which thou considerest the evil consequences of corruption, the effects of wrongs and evils... The fifth meditation is the meditation on serenity, in which thou risest above love and hate, tyranny and thraldom, wealth and want, and regardest thine own fate with impartial calmness and perfect tranquillity."[183]

Buddha, *The Gospel of Buddha*, LX.

SECOND STEP – FOCUS ON LOVING-KINDNESS

The essence of spirituality is love—to express loving-kindness for all created things, which allows us to be at one with all things. As we are all component parts of a greater whole, so are we all mirrors of the Divine Being which brought all things into existence. As we mirror His eternal attributes, so do we act as conduits of love and compassion to all contingent beings. As Nukariya writes: "Our bliss consists in seeing the fragrant rose of Divine mercy among the thorns of worldly trouble, in finding the fair oasis of Buddha's wisdom in the desert of misfortunes, in getting the wholesome balm of His love in the seeming poison of pain, in gathering the sweet honey of His spirit even in the sting of horrible death."[184]

Our happiness can transcend all physical limitations and suffering, because it is spiritual happiness. The fruit of happiness is loving-kindness. Can we be happy while we cause suffering to others? Can we become happy through cruelty? Can we become happy by accumulating wealth at the expense of others?—or, rather, are we happy when we act magnanimously and generously, giving of the excess of our income to others? Happiness, therefore, depends on the expression of loving-kindness to all things and all living beings.

The purpose of loving-kindness meditation is to keep our minds open and sweet.[185] We should learn to develop kindness, not just to others, but to ourselves as well. We should try not to feel unworthy or dejected. Rather, we should recognize our own inner nobility. We are all oceans full of great value—great treasures hidden in the profoundest depths. We should avoid all feelings of negativity, self-loathing and self-doubt, all tendencies towards 'beating ourselves up' and feelings of worthlessness. We are spiritual beings—we are eternal beings—we are souls created in the image of the Higher Being which fashioned us—the All-Highest Being, the All-Knowing, the All-Wise.

In Pali, loving-kindness meditation is referred to as *metta bhavana*, with *metta* meaning love (i.e. spiritual love, rather than passion) and *bhavana*, which means development or cultivation.[186] According to the Buddhist practice of loving-kindness meditation, we should develop loving-kindness towards four types of people: respected individuals (e.g. a spiritual teacher), beloved individuals (e.g. close family and friends), neutral individuals (e.g. people whom we know but have no special feelings towards), and hostile individuals (e.g. people we are at conflict with or with whom we are having difficulties).[187] Ways to develop loving-kindness include visualization (i.e. seeing a mental picture of the other person smiling at you or being joyful), reflection on the positive qualities of a person and the kind acts they have done towards you, and auditory (i.e. repeating a positive phrase to yourself, such as 'loving-kindness').[188] This practice should be divided into five stages, each lasting about five minutes for a complete beginner.[189] These are the steps:

Feel loving-kindness for yourself. Be aware of your own being and focus on the peace and tranquility within you. You can focus on an image, such as light pouring through your inner being. Next, think of a good friend and feel your connection to him/her. Fill yourself with good wishes for that person, silently repeating, for example: 'May he/she be happy.' Third, think of someone you do not particularly like (or dislike) and reflect on their inner nobility. Feel loving-kindness towards them. Fourth, think of someone you dislike, i.e. your enemy. Think of them in a positive way and feel loving-kindness towards them. Lastly, think of all four individuals together and then extend the circle of loving-kindness outwards, embracing the whole of humanity with your love. Extend your loving-kindness from your local community, to your region, your nation and, finally, the entire world and universe.[190] In short:

- We should act as conduits of love and compassion to all contingent beings
- We should recognize our own inner nobility
- The practice of loving-kindness meditation is divided into five stages.
- First, focus on loving yourself
- Second, focus on loving a friend or other loved one
- Third, focus on loving someone whom you neither like nor dislike
- Fourth, focus on loving someone whom you dislike
- Lastly, focus on loving all four individuals together and then extend your love to your community, region, nation, the world and the universe

"Amitābha, the unbounded light, is the source of wisdom, of virtue, of Buddhahood. The deeds of sorcerers and miracle-mongers are frauds, but what is more wondrous, more mysterious, more miraculous than Amitābha?... the repetition of the name Amitābha Buddha is meritorious only if thou speak it with such a devout attitude of mind as will cleanse thy heart and attune thy will to do works of righteousness."[191]

- Buddha, *The Gospel of Buddha*, LX.

THIRD STEP – MANTRA MEDITATION

The third method of meditation is mantra meditation. A mantra is a word or phrase which has special power that is repeated again and again in the process of meditation. Examples include the word Amitābha, the Buddha of Unbounded Light, who dwells in a realm called the 'Pure Land'. He is also called Amita or Amida Buddha, and he is the centre of devotion for the Pure Land Buddhism school of Mahayana Buddhism.[192] Amitābha literally means 'Infinite Light', while his alternative title of Amitāyus means 'Infinite Life'.[193] Yejitsu Okusa, in *Principal Teachings of The True Sect of Pure Land*, writes: "In the True Sect of Pure Land, we have the true, all-embracing love of Amida to save all beings from ignorance and pain. It is the net of boundless compassion thrown by the Buddha's own hand into the sea of misery, in which the ignorant rather than the wise, the sinful rather than the good, are meant to be gathered up. This love and compassion is eternally abiding with the Buddha, whose will to save all beings knows no temporal limitations; and on this account the Buddha is called *Amitāyus* (Eternal Life). His power to save is manifest in his light..."[194] It is clear from this description that Amitābha is not a person, but the Primal Will, the Higher Power which creates and sustains all things.

Furthermore, by focusing on Amitābha, one actually attains to true Enlightenment and Paradise, as Okusa explains: "Those who have awakened this faith in the love of Amida which saves, are at once embraced in his light and destined to be born in Pure Land after death. This light is the will of Amida under whose merciful care all beings are made to grow; it reaches every part of the universe, knowing no spatial limitations. Therefore, the Buddha is also called *Amitābha* (Infinite Light). His will to save is, thus, infinite not only in time but in space, hence his two attributes, Amitāyus and Amitābha... Amida is the Father of all beings; he is the Only One; he has, from the very beginning of all things, been contriving to save the world..."[195] In the *Amitāyus-sūtra*, He states: "I will make every one enjoy a rebirth in Pure Land if he listen to my name and believe in my will to save and rejoice in it."[196] This is very similar to the Christian concept of salvation through faith in Jesus Christ, who says: "I am the way, the truth, and the life: no man cometh unto the Father, but by me."[197]

In Sanskrit, the mantra invoking Amitābha is: **Om amitābha hrīh**,[198] or **Namo Amitābhāya**.[199] The Japanese version of the latter mantra is **Namu Amida Butsu**, and in Mandarin Chinese, it is **Nāmó Ēmítuófó**.[200] One can choose whichever form is easiest to say, as each has the same effect. Some examples on YouTube can be found here (https://www.youtube.com/watch?v=30kgbA3Ib7k), here (https://www.youtube.com/watch?v=3FS7YPSbHNk), here (https://www.youtube.com/watch?v=vWXlPGEeeSI), and here

(https://www.youtube.com/watch?v=kEQ2xAQ6tMQ).
All of these mantras are one and the same, all calling
on Amitābha as the Primal Will of our Creator, so that
we can achieve Enlightenment and enter the realm of
Paradise in the world to come. Okusa writes: "While
all other deeds of ours are more or less defiled, the
reciting of 'Namu Amida Bu' is an act free from
impurities; for it is not we that recite it, but Amida
himself, who, giving us his own name, makes us recite
it."[201]

Another divine Name which is often used in
mantra meditation is the Name of Krishna, the Great
Teacher who appeared in India after the time of Rāma
but before the time of Gautama Buddha. In the
Mahābharata, the greatest epic tale of ancient India,
he enumerates a number of his names and attributes,
all of which are also Names and Attributes of the
Divine, as he was a pure Mirror of the Divine Being.
He says, for instance, "I till the Earth, assuming the
form of a large plough-share of black iron. And
because my complexion is black, therefore am I called
by the name of Krishna. I have united the Earth with
Water, Space with Mind, and Wind with Light.
Therefore am I called Vaikuntha..."[202] The names and

titles of Krishna are too numerous to list here. However, one popular mantra, popularized by the 16th century Hindu teacher, Sri Chaitanya Mahaprabhu, was the recitation of the Hare Krishna mantra: *Hare Krishna, Hare Krishna / Krishna, Krishna, Hare Hare / Hare Rāma, Hare Rāma / Rāma Rāma, Hare Hare.* This mantra invokes Krishna and Rāma, both Hindu Avatars, or Manifestations of the Divine, as well as the vocative form of the name Hari,[203] which means 'He who removes illusion.'[204] It is useful to use *japa*-beads while repeating the names.[205] There are usually 108 beads of each set. Further advice on chanting the mantra can be found at Krishna.com and here: http://www.iskcon.org/meditation/. You can listen to examples of the mantra on YouTube here (https://www.youtube.com/watch?v=eban9M_Sdk4) and here (https://www.youtube.com/watch?v=_oDxBfin5zg).

Other methods include the repetition of the Arabic names of God, such as *Allāh*, which simply means 'God' in Arabic, or *Ya-llāh* ('O God'), *Yā 'Ilāhī* ('O my God'), or the many other names of God mentioned in the Qur'ān, such as *Ar-Rahmān* (the 'Most Merciful'), *Ar-Rahīm* (the 'Merciful'), *Dhu l-*

Jalāl-i wa l-Ikrām (the 'Possessor of Glory and Bounty'), etc. Another Arabic invocation of God is *Allāhumma*, which is another way of saying 'O God'. In the Qur'ān, God says—glorified be His Glory: "SAY: Call upon God (*Allāh*), or call upon the God of Mercy (*Arrahmān*), by whichsoever ye will invoke him: He hath most excellent names. And be not loud in thy prayer, neither pronounce it too low but between these follow a middle way."[206] The mystic poet, Rūmī, writes: "They are names derived from God's essential attributes, not mere vain titles of the First Cause. For if so, they would be only empty pleasantries, like calling the deaf a hearer and the blind a seer..."[207] Examples of Islamic chants can be found here (https://www.youtube.com/watch?v=KTdDXnWj8JE) and here (https://www.youtube.com/watch?v=mrcoYTGCXvc). Additional mantras and invocations may be found in the Jewish, Christian and other traditions. In summary:

- A mantra is a word or phrase which has special power that is repeated many times in the process of meditation

- One of the most powerful Buddhist mantras is to recite the name of Amitābha Buddha
- This can be chanted in any language (whichever is easier for the reciter)
- Another name that can be used is that of Krishna, who had many attributes
- The Hare Krishna mantra can be recited using *japa*-beads
- The various Arabic Names of God can be used, as well as various Qur'ānic invocations
- Other invocations can be found in the Jewish and Christian scriptures and religious literature

"A blessed Book have we sent down to thee, that men may meditate its verses, and that those endued with understanding may bear it in mind."[208]

- Qur'ān 38:29

FOURTH STEP – MEDITATION ON THE WORD

This method involves contemplation on the Divine Word as revealed by the Great Teachers of the past, such as Gautama Buddha, Krishna, Zoroaster,

Moses, and Muhammad (may peace be upon all of them). Thomas à Kempis advised: "It is Truth which we must look for in Holy Writ, not cunning of words. All Scripture ought to be read in the spirit in which it was written. We must rather seek for what is profitable in Scripture, than for what ministereth to subtlety in discourse. Therefore, we ought to read books which are devotional and simple, as well as those which are deep and difficult."[209] He thus advises meditation on all parts of the Bible, aiming to understand the text in the spirit in which it was written, rather than imposing our own ideas on its meanings or taking it out of context. He also says: "Men pass away, but the truth of the Lord endureth for ever. Without respect of persons God speaketh to us in divers manners. Our own curiosity often hindereth us in the reading of holy writings, when we seek to understand and discuss, where we should pass simply on. If thou wouldst profit by thy reading, read humbly, simply, honestly, and not desiring to win a character for learning. Ask freely, and hear in silence the words of holy men; nor be displeased at the hard sayings of older men than thou, for they are not uttered without cause."[210]

This is simplicity itself. We should read these Holy Books in a patient and open manner, avoiding imposing our own interpretations on the text, while also not taking the texts too literally. Some of these texts, after all, have been passed down through oral traditions and may have undergone textual changes over time. The Qur'ān, being the most recent of the ones mentioned above, is incredibly accurate, as it was recorded within a generation of the Prophet's passing. Some of the Biblical books, however, were written down centuries after the original composition, e.g. in the case of the Torah. The New Testament letters of Paul were preserved and copied, but the Gospel stories of Jesus Christ were written down decades after Christ's crucifixion, and were recorded in Greek, which was not the language spoken by Christ (who spoke Aramaic and Hebrew). We should also bear in mind that many of the Great Teachers and Prophets spoke in parables, using symbolic language. Symbolic language was used because many of the listeners at the time did not have the spiritual capacity to understand the teachings without using symbols. Life, for example, means 'spiritual life', rather than physical life. Resurrection means attaining spiritual life, rather than literal resurrection of bodies, etc. Therefore, we should not take what these Great Teachers and Prophets have said literally, and should try to understand them in the original context. Thus, Jesus said: "Therefore speak I to them in parables: because they seeing see not; and hearing they hear not, neither do they understand."[211]

It is best not to read too much every day but to focus on a small sample of scripture or a small passage. This verse from the Qur'ān, for instance, is particularly powerful and moving: "**And whoso feareth God, to him will He grant a prosperous issue, and will provide for him whence he reckoned not upon it. And for him who putteth his trust in Him will God be all-sufficient. God truly will attain his purpose. For everything hath God assigned a period.**"[212] Another beautiful verse is called the Light verse, where God says: "**God is the LIGHT of the Heavens and of the Earth. His Light is like a niche in which is a lamp - the lamp encased in glass - the glass, as it were, a glistening star. From a blessed tree is it lighted, the olive neither of the East nor of the West, whose oil would well nigh shine out,** even though fire touched it not! It is light upon light. God guideth whom He will to His light, and God setteth forth parables to men, for God knoweth all things."[213]

Another beautiful passage is the Beatitudes of Jesus Christ, which he uttered on the Mount of Olives. It forms part of the Sermon on the Mount, which is the essence of Christian teaching:

> "Blessed are the poor in spirit: for theirs is the kingdom of heaven. Blessed are they that mourn: for they shall be comforted. Blessed are the meek: for they shall inherit the earth. Blessed are they which do hunger and thirst after righteousness: for they shall be filled. Blessed are the merciful: for they shall obtain mercy. Blessed are the pure in heart: for they shall see God. Blessed are the peacemakers: for they shall be called the children of God. Blessed are they which are persecuted for righteousness' sake: for theirs is the kingdom of heaven. Blessed are ye, when men shall revile you, and persecute you, and shall say all manner of evil against you falsely, for my sake. Rejoice, and be exceeding glad: for great is your reward in heaven: for so persecuted they the prophets which were before you."[214]

Jesus then goes on to say: **"Ye are the salt of the earth: but if the salt have lost his savour, wherewith shall it be salted? it is thenceforth good for nothing, but to be cast out, and to be trodden under foot of men. Ye are the light of the world. A city that is set on an hill cannot be hid. Neither do men light a candle, and put it under a bushel, but on a candlestick; and it giveth light unto all that are in the house. Let your light so shine before men, that they may see your good works, and glorify your Father which is in heaven."**[215] You may want to write some of these verses in a notebook, so that you can memorize them or repeat them often in your daily meditations and contemplation on the Word of God. The Word of God is an unlimited source of power and strength, of knowledge and wisdom. As God says in the Qur'ān, glorified be He: **"SAY: Should the sea become ink, to write the words of my Lord, the sea would surely fail ere the words of my Lord would fail, though we brought its like in aid."**[216] Memorizing this verse will also aid you in raising your level of spiritual awareness. In short:

- We should meditate on the Divine word as revealed by the Great Teachers and Prophets of the past
- We should read the scriptures in order to find the Truth
- We should read verses in the spirit in which they are written, trying to understand the context
- We should not take scriptures too literally
- We should try to read in a spirit of humbleness, honesty and simplicity, and with a desire to learn
- We should memorize certain verses and repeat them often
- We can write particularly powerful verses which we like in a notebook to help us in our continual reflections and meditations

∞∞∞∞∞∞∞∞∞∞∞∞∞∞∞∞∞∞∞∞∞∞∞∞

"My God, my all! To him that understandeth, that word sufficeth, and to repeat it often is pleasing to him that loveth it. When Thou art present all things are pleasant; when Thou art absent, all things are wearisome. Thou makest the heart to be at rest, givest it deep peace and festal joy. Thou makest it to think rightly in every matter, and in every matter to give Thee praise; neither can anything please long without Thee but if it would be pleasant and of sweet savour, Thy grace must be there, and it is Thy wisdom which must give unto it a sweet savour."[217]

- Thomas à Kempis, *The Imitation of Christ*, Ch. XXXIV

FIFTH STEP – MEDITATION ON THE DIVINE

The fifth type of meditation we will mention here is meditation on the Divine. This means, essentially, meditation on God and His attributes. It is similar to mantra meditation, but without the actual recitation of an audible sound. In this state, we meditate on the sublimity of the Divine Being and His attributes, and commune with our spirits. As Thomas à Kempis remarks: "He to whom the Eternal Word speaketh is free from multiplied questionings. From this One Word are all things, and all things speak of Him; and

this is the Beginning which also speaketh unto us."[218]
In the Qur'ān, God gives numerous examples of things
on which mankind should meditate or reflect. For
example:

> "SAY: Whose is the earth, and all that is
> therein;—if ye know? They will answer,
> 'God's.' SAY: Will ye not, then reflect?
>
> "SAY: Who is the Lord of the seven
> heavens, and the Lord of the glorious
> throne? They will say, 'They are God's'.
> SAY: Will ye not, then, fear Him?
>
> "SAY: In whose hand is the empire of all
> things, who protecteth but is not
> protected? if ye know: They will answer,
> 'In God's.' SAY: How, then, can ye be so
> spell-bound?... God hath not begotten
> offspring; neither is there any other God
> with Him."[219]

William Penn, who was a prominent early Quaker,
wrote some advice to his children. He advised them to
meditate in the morning, in silence, and lift up their
hearts to him. He wrote: "So soon as you wake, retire
your mind into a pure silence from all thoughts and
ideas of worldly things, and in that frame wait upon
GOD, to feel His good presence, to lift up your hearts

to Him, and commit your whole self into his blessed care and protection."[220] In the Bhagavad-Gita, Krishna urges his disciple, Arjuna, who was about to fight a great battle, to meditate on the Divine, which should always be within his heart. He says: "Have Me, then, in thy heart always! and fight! Thou too, when heart and mind are fixed on Me, shalt surely come to Me! All come who cleave with never-wavering will of firmest faith, owning none other Gods: all come to Me, the Uttermost, Purusha, Holiest!"[221] In the same book, he also explains some of the attributes of God, which we can meditate upon, along with His Divine Names. He says:

"He is within all beings—and without— motionless, yet still moving; not discerned for subtlety of instant presence; close to all, to each; yet measurelessly far! Not manifold, and yet subsisting still in all which lives; for ever to be known as the Sustainer, yet, at the End of Times, He maketh all to end—and re-creates. The Light of Lights He is, in the heart of the Dark Shining eternally. Wisdom He is and Wisdom's way, and Guide of all the wise, planted in every heart."[222]

One should meditate on the many attributes of God and His sublimity, as well as our inner nobility, seeing our hearts as mirrors of the Divine and the Light of God which shines within the heart and inner being of each and every person. In short:

- We should sit in silence and commune with the Divine without speaking
- We should meditate on God's power and might
- We should meditate on God's attributes
- We should meditate in the mornings, lifting up our hearts to God
- We would remember God's nearness and His sublimity
- We should remember our own inner nobility and the Light of God which shines within us

Questions for Reflection:

The following are some questions that will help us to reflect on what we have learned in this chapter:

1. What is Zazen and how should we practise Zen meditation?
2. What is loving-kindness and how should we practise loving-kindness meditation?
3. How should we meditate on the Word?

4. What are some mantras we can chant during mantra meditation?

5. What are some ways we can meditate on the Divine?

In the next chapter, we will look at the Fifth Way to Be—Enkindlement.

∞∞∞∞∞∞∞∞∞∞∞∞∞∞∞∞∞∞∞∞∞∞∞

XIII. FIFTH WAY TO BE – ENKINDLEMENT

Parable:

"Moreover, Son of Pandu! wert thou worst

Of all wrong-doers, this fair ship of Truth

Should bear thee safe and dry across the sea

Of thy transgressions. As the kindled flame

Feeds on the fuel till it sinks to ash,

So unto ash, Arjuna! unto nought

The flame of Knowledge wastes works' dross away!

There is no purifier like thereto

In all this world, and he who seeketh it

Shall find it—being grown perfect—in himself.

Believing, he receives it when the soul

Masters itself, and cleaves to Truth, and comes—

Possessing knowledge—to the higher peace,

The uttermost repose.'"[223]

- Krishna, *The Bhagavad-Gita*, Chapter IV.

Reflections:

In the parable above, Krishna is speaking to his friend and devotee, Arjuna, on the battlefield. Krishna likens the Truth to a ship which carries one across the sea of one's transgressions. Our sins or misdeeds, even if they are as numerous as an ocean, can easily be overcome and transcended through the ship of the Truth, which is the ship of salvation. Confucius said: "They who know the truth are not equal to those who love it, and they who love it are not equal to those who delight in it."[224] Likewise, in the Qur'ān, God says—glorified be He: "SAY: Shall they who have knowledge and they who have it not, be treated alike? In sooth, men of understanding only will take the warning."[225] What is this Truth that Krishna speaks of? He tells Arjuna: "Of many thousand mortals, one, perchance, striveth for Truth; and of those few that strive—Nay, and rise high—one only—here and there—knoweth Me, as I am, the very Truth."[226] The ultimate Truth, then, is to recognize that the Truth is not an abstract concept or an unattainable goal—rather, the ultimate Truth is the Creative Force, the Higher Being which brought all of creation into being, and that Truth is manifest in the Person of those Great Beings, those Great Teachers and Messengers of God who appear in the world and give us divine teachings.

As we have mentioned in previous chapters, we should recognize the Light in whatever Lamp it appears. If we recognize the Light of Krishna, we should also recognize the Light of Buddha, and the Light of Moses, and the Light of Christ, and the Light of Muhammad, because they are one Light, though the Lamps are different. In the Qur'ān, He says: "The apostle believeth in that which hath been sent down from his Lord, as do the faithful also. Each one believeth in God, and His Angels, and His Books, and His Apostles: we make no distinction between any of His Apostles. And they say, 'We have heard and we obey. Thy mercy, Lord! for unto thee must we return.'"[227] It is with humility that we must accept that we do not know what is best ourselves. We have to humbly accept that there is a higher knowledge and that we must accept that knowledge from the correct source, which is God, who gives knowledge to the Great Teachers—the Messengers who appear from time to time throughout history. Speaking to those who opposed the Prophet Muhammad, God says: "Lo! ye are they who dispute about that in which ye have knowledge; but why dispute ye about that of which ye have no knowledge? God hath knowledge, but ye know nothing."[228]

"When love of God kindles a flame in the inward man,

He burns, and is freed from effects.

He has no need of signs to assure him of Love,

For Love casts its own Light up to heaven."[229]

- Rumi, *The Masnavi*

Next, Krishna tells Arjuna: "As the kindled flame feeds on the fuel till it sinks to ash, so unto ash, Arjuna! unto nought the flame of Knowledge wastes works' dross away!" What is the kindled flame? Here, this refers to knowledge—true knowledge, divine knowledge—which burns away the fuel of desire and passion and purifies the heart. The flame of knowledge burns our impurities and imperfections away until all that is left is the pure flame of Truth which burns brightly in the midmost centre of one's heart—the temple of our inner beings. This is the goal of devotion and the whole aim of religion and spirituality—to kindle the light of Truth and burn away our own egos and selfish desires. As George Fox, the founder of the Religious Society of Friends (known as Quakers), has advised: "And all my dear Friends, dwell in the life, and love, and power, and wisdom of God, in unity one with another, and with God; and the peace and wisdom of God fill all your hearts that nothing may rule in you but the life which stands in the Lord God."[230]

The true reality of divine knowledge is love and attraction. The highest knowledge is to feel absolute love for the Absolute, to fill ourselves with a desperate, burning love for the Divine, and to destroy our egos which prevent us from approaching the Divine. We must burn away all earthly passion and desire and draw our hearts towards that one Light which shines brightly through every veil and obstacle. It is an eternal Light which can pierce the innermost essence of our hearts and fill us with the water of life. While yet young, George Fox (1624 – 1691), who lived in England in the 17th century, came to a realization that God was not some abstract being which lived in a church or temple. He realized that God "did not dwell in these temples which men had commanded and set up, but in people's hearts."[231] On one occasion, having returned home after walking for a while, he had an immense experience of divine love. He writes: "I was taken up in the love of God, so that I could not but admire the greatness of His love; and while l was in that condition, it was opened unto me by the eternal light and power... I saw, also, that there was an ocean of darkness and death; but an infinite ocean of light and love, which flowed over the ocean of darkness. In that also I saw the infinite love of God, and I had great openings."[232]

> **"Human perfection resides in this, that the love of God should conquer a man's heart and possess it wholly, and even if it does not possess it wholly it should predominate in the heart over the love of all other things."[233]**
> - Al-Ghazali, *The Alchemy of Happiness*, Ch. VIII.

The love of God is the highest love and the greatest reality for, as the Bible says (1 John 4:16): "He that loveth not knoweth not God; for God is love."[234] Later in the same book, we read: "And we have known and believed the love that God hath to us. God is love; and he that dwelleth in love dwelleth in God, and God in him."[235] To love God, we must be renounced and submitted to God, so that the Light of God can dwell within us. Krishna says: "Do all thou dost for Me! Renounce for Me! Sacrifice heart and mind and will to Me! Live in the faith of Me! In faith of Me all dangers thou shalt vanquish, by My grace; but, trusting to thyself and heeding not, thou can'st but perish!"[236]

It is necessary, then, to focus our hearts and wills on the Will of God, which is true detachment. We must live in a state of faith and prayer, which will lead us to the ship of salvation, the ship of knowledge, which will take us across the sea of misery and despair, the sea of our own misdeeds, to that other shore—the spiritual realm of eternity. Only by kindling the fire of the love of God in our hearts, can we burn away all vain imaginings and illusions, and achieve a state of true happiness and eternal felicity and joy.

"I saw into that which was without end, things which cannot be uttered, and of the greatness and infinitude of the love of God, which cannot be expressed by words."[237]

- George Fox, *An Autobiography*, Chapter I.

This love of God is compared to a fire, because fire burns away everything else that comes into contact with it. If the fire of love burns in your heart, then everything else which comes your way, whether ego or self-interest or other desires and selfish goals are burned up by the flames of that fire. Al-Ghazali writes: "In truth, if the love of God really take possession of the heart all other love is excluded."[238] Likewise, however, there is a danger that the fire will die down and be blown out. In such a case, the fire will need to be reignited. The question is, then, how do we kindle this fire and how do we maintain a state of enkindlement? The Persian mystic poet Hafez writes: "If thou would'st know the secret of Love's fire, it shall be manifest unto thine eyes: question the torch flame burning steadfastly, but ask no more the sweet wind's wayward choir. Ask me of faith and love that never dies; Darius, Alexander's sovereignty, I sing of these no more."[239] The key is to set out on the path of enkindlement, by the following the Four Ways which have already been mentioned. If we follow each of these steps, we become detached, radiantly acquiescent, magnanimous, and contemplative; then we can easily achieve the next stage of enkindlement, because everything is in place. The wood has been collected and put in place before the campfire is ready to be ignited. All that is required is the spark of love. As St. Augustine prayed:

> **"O Lord, my God, give me what Thou biddest and then bid what Thou wilt!... For he loves Thee but little who loves other things with Thee, and loves them not for Thee! O Love that ever burnest and wilt never be extinguished! O Charity! O Lord, my God, set me on fire! Thou dost bid continence? Then give me what Thou biddest and bid what Thou wilt!"[240]**

Questions for Reflection:

The following are some questions that will help us to reflect on what we have learned in this chapter:

1. What will enable us to overcome our misdeeds and reach the shores of spiritual happiness?

2. Where can we find divine knowledge? Who will give it to us?

3. What do we need to do for the Light of God to dwell within us?

4. What state must we live in?

5. What practices must we maintain before we can reach a state of enkindlement?

In the next chapter, we will look at some practical ways to achieve enkindlement.

∞∞∞∞∞∞∞∞∞∞∞∞∞∞∞∞∞∞∞∞∞∞∞∞

XIV. THE FIFTH PRACTICE – FASTING OF THE HEART

"Love is the seed of happiness, and love to God is fostered and developed by worship."[241]

- Al-Ghazālī, *The Alchemy of Happiness*, Chapter II.

One of the disciples of Confucius, called Yen Hui (also known as Tzu Yuan), asked his Master how he could achieve success when he was to go and instruct the Prince of Wei. He asked for a method to lead him to a state of true spiritual enkindlement. "Fast," Confucius urged him. Yen Hui replied: "Well, my family is poor, and for many months we have tasted neither wine nor flesh. Is not that fasting?" "The fasting of religious observance it is," Confucius replied. "But not the fasting of the heart." Confused, Yen Hui asked what the fasting of the heart was. "Cultivate unity," Confucius replied. "You hear not with the ears, but with the mind; not with the mind, but with your soul. But let hearing stop with the ears. Let the working of the mind stop with itself. Then the soul will be a negative existence, passively responsive to externals. In such a negative existence, only TAO can abide. And that negative state is the fasting of the heart." Yen Hui suddenly realized the essence of his problem. "The reason I could not get the use of this method," he remarked, "is my own individuality. If I could get the use of it, my individuality would have gone. Is this what you mean by the negative state?"242

"Exactly so," Confucius replied. "Let me tell you. If you can enter this man's domain without offending his *amour propre*,2 cheerful if he hears you, passive if he does not; without science, without drugs, simply living there in a state of complete indifference,—you will be near success. It is easy to stop walking: the trouble is to walk without touching the ground. As an agent of man, it is easy to deceive; but not as an agent of God. You have heard of winged creatures flying. You have never heard of flying without wings. You have heard of men being wise with wisdom. You have never heard of men wise without wisdom. Look at that window. Through it an empty room becomes bright with scenery; but the landscape stops outside. Were this not so, we should have an exemplification of sitting still and running away at one and the same

---

2 His own sense of self-worth.

time. In this sense, you may use your ears and eyes to communicate within, but shut out all wisdom from the mind. And there where the supernatural can find shelter, shall not man find shelter also? This is the method for regenerating all creation... Shall it not then be adopted by mankind in general?"[243]

"He is always ready, indeed, to give us His light, not, indeed, His visible light, but the light of the intellect and the spirit. It is we who are not always prepared to receive it, and this because we are preoccupied with other things and swallowed up in the darkness resulting from desire of the things of earth."[244]
- St. Thomas Aquinas, *On Prayer and the Contemplative Life*, Question LXXXIII

The essence of this tale, which was reported by the great Chinese philosopher, Zhuang Zhou (also known as Zhuangzi), is that we should so empty ourselves of the insistent self within, becoming a pure vessel of Truth, that the TAO may abide within our hearts. In other words, our hearts, like a pure mirror, should reflect the Light of Truth within. Then the fire of love will be kindled in our hearts and we will consume all vanity and vain desires. This, according to Confucius, is 'fasting of the heart'. It is fasting, not from physical food and drink, useful as that is as a practice, but from attachment to all things, including our own individuality. We should become like an empty room, bright with the light of the external world, but free from attachment to that which surrounds it. This is what it means 'to walk without touching the ground.' He says that if we communicate within (e.g. through meditation), then the supernatural, i.e. the Divine, can find shelter in the innermost essence of our hearts. Then will we find true shelter and happiness. Confucius says: "To serve one's own heart so as to permit neither joy nor sorrow within, but to cultivate resignation to the inevitable,— this is the climax of Virtue."245

According to Zhuangzi, the object of all learning— all knowledge—is the knowledge of God. He writes: "He who knows what God is, and who knows what Man is, has attained. Knowing what God is, he knows that he himself proceeded therefrom. Knowing what Man is, he rests in the knowledge of the known, waiting for the knowledge of the unknown... God is a principle which exists by virtue of its own intrinsicality, and operates spontaneously, without self-manifestation."[246] True knowledge, he argued, however, could only come of pure men. And pure men were those who were aware of the oneness of the material world and the oneness of the Source of their being, which is God. "For what they cared for could be reduced to ONE," Zhuangzi writes, "and what they did not care for to ONE also. That which was ONE was ONE, and that which was not ONE was likewise ONE. In that which was ONE, they were of God; in that which was not ONE, they were of Man. And so between the human and the divine no conflict ensued. This was to be a pure man. Life and Death belong to Destiny. Their sequence, like day and night, is of God, beyond the interference of man, an inevitable law... A man looks upon a ruler of men as upon some one better than himself, for whom he would sacrifice his life. Shall he not then do so for the Supreme Ruler of Creation?"[247]

"And what have we to do with talk about genus and species! He to whom the Eternal Word speaketh is free from multiplied questionings. From this One Word are all things, and all things speak of Him; and this is the Beginning which also speaketh

unto us. No man without Him understandeth or rightly judgeth. The man to whom all things are one, who bringeth all things to one, who seeth all things in one, he is able to remain steadfast of spirit, and at rest in God. O God, who art the Truth, make me one with Thee in everlasting love. It wearieth me oftentimes to read and listen to many things; in Thee is all that I wish for and desire. Let all the doctors hold their peace; let all creation keep silence before Thee: speak Thou alone to me."248

- Thomas à Kempis, *The Imitation of Christ*, Chapter III

All of this may seem rather abstract, but it conveys deep, spiritual meanings. The sum of it is this: the object of all knowledge is God. Pure men, i.e. those who have reached the highest level of purity and knowledge of God, are aware of the oneness of the Divine Being and that which is not the Divine Being, i.e. creation. That which is not the One Creator is material and changeable, while the One itself, i.e. God, is self-subsisting and exists by virtue of its own Being, Uncreated, Unborn and Unformed. When we free ourselves from the fetters of this material world, we allow that Divine Oneness, that Divine Being, to fill us with His Light and Truth. If we do that, then we can transcend fear and material attachment and become truly free, enkindled with the love of God and the flame of true knowledge and true existence. This is the real life of the soul. As Confucius says: "By nourishment of physical courage, the sense of fear may be so eliminated that a man will, singlehanded, brave a whole army. And if such a result can be achieved in search of fame, how much more by one who extends his sway over heaven and earth and influences all things; and who, lodging within the confines of a body with its channels of sight and sound, brings his knowledge to know that all things are ONE, and that his soul endures for ever!"[249]

> **"O men! now hath a proof come to you from your Lord, and we have sent down to you a clear light. As to those who believe in God and lay fast hold on Him, these will He cause to enter into his mercy and grace, and along the straight way unto Himself will He guide them."[250]**
>
> - Qur'ān 4:174

The practical method of achievement of this is, first of all, to practice the previous 'Ways to Be' mentioned in this book, viz. Detachment, Radiant

Acquiescence, Magnanimity, and Contemplation. These are the gateways that lead to the final stage of Enkindlement, which is also called Enlightenment. This is the true Straight Path, the Middle Way spoken of in the Buddhist Scriptures. This is the true Way of the TAO (or DAO) and the Path to the Divine. This is the Way which Jesus spoke of when he said: "I am the way, the truth, and the life: no man cometh unto the Father, but by me. If ye had known me, ye should have known my Father also: and from henceforth ye know him, and have seen him."251 Likewise, in the Gospel of John, Jesus says: "I am the door: by me if any man enter in, he shall be saved, and shall go in and out, and find pasture."252 As the pure Manifestation of the Way, as the Pure Mirror of the Divine, Jesus Christ was the Gate through which all could enter onto the Straight Path and follow the true Teachings of Truth and Life, thus achieving true mindfulness, equanimity and enkindlement with the fire of the love of God.

Next, one must practice the 'fasting of the heart' which Confucius refers to. This means emptying oneself of one's own individuality and allowing the Light of God to shine within us. It means achieving a true state of stillness and equanimity. Confucius says: "A man does not seek to see himself in running water, but in still water. For only what is itself still can instil stillness into others."[253] Meditation and contemplation are the key to achieving this state of stillness in one's inner being. The daily devotional practices of prayer and meditation are keys to achieving a perpetual state of equanimity. Emptying ourselves of selfishness and ego, this will allow our hearts to be flooded with the power of the Divine. Confucius calls this 'feeding upon the Divine.' He says: "And those who thus feed upon the divine have little need for the human. They wear the forms of men, without human passions. Because they wear the forms of men, they associate with men. Because they have not human passions, positives and negatives find in them no place. Infinitesimal indeed is that which makes them man: infinitely great is that which makes them divine!"[254]

"It is by our acts that we merit. But devotion has a peculiarly meritorious character. Consequently devotion is a special kind of act. Devotion is so termed from 'devoting' oneself. Hence the 'devout' are so named because they 'devote'

themselves to God and thus proclaim their complete subjection to Him."[255]

- St. Thomas Aquinas, *On Prayer and the Contemplative Life*, Question LXXXII.

Thus, we should, through devotional practices, try to refine our inner selves and become absorbed in the love of God above all things. We must abstain from that which is lower in order to achieve that which is higher, through following the Eightfold Path outlined by the Buddha, by remembering the impermanence of all things, by remembering that all things are subject to change and dissolution, by abstaining from alcohol and other intoxicants, as well as abstaining from and avoiding sexual immorality, gossip and backbiting, gambling, theft, and harmfulness to all living creatures. This will help to purify our hearts. We should absorb ourselves in daily prayer and meditation, contemplation on the sacred writings and scriptures of the ages, and try to live out their teachings in our lives. Then we will be able to transcend our lower selves and become absorbed in the love of God. Then we will be able to develop the qualities and characteristics of true humanity. As Al-Ghazali has written: "For perfect happiness mere knowledge is not enough, unaccompanied by love, and the love of God cannot take possession of a man's heart till it be purified from love of the world, which purification can only be effected by abstinence and austerity."[256]

In the next chapter, we will look at some practical Steps to Achieve a State of Enkindlement.

Questions for Reflection:

The following are some questions that will help us to reflect on what we have learned in this chapter:

1. What is 'fasting of the heart'?
2. How can we transcend fear and become truly free?
3. What does Confucius mean by 'feeding upon the Divine'?
4. What are some examples of things we should abstain from in order to purify our hearts?
5. What should we absorb ourselves in, in order to achieve true equanimity and happiness?

∞∞∞∞∞∞∞∞∞∞∞∞∞∞∞∞∞∞∞∞∞∞∞∞

XV. FASTING OF THE HEART – STEPS FOR FURTHER DEVELOPMENT

The following are some practical steps for further development in the practice of enkindling love for the Divine within our hearts.

> "Know, O beloved, that man was not created in jest or at random, but marvellously made and for some great end. Although he is not from everlasting, yet he lives for ever; and though his body is mean and earthly, yet his spirit is lofty and divine. When in the crucible of abstinence he is purged from carnal passions he attains to the highest and in place of being a slave to lust and anger becomes endued with angelic qualities. Attaining that state, he finds his heaven in the contemplation of Eternal Beauty, and no longer in fleshly delights."[257]
>
> - Al-Ghazali, *The Alchemy of Happiness*, Introduction

STEP 1 – FAST REGULARLY

Fasting is a useful method for developing detachment and cleansing the spirit from impurity and impure attachments. It involves physically regulating ourselves in order to develop our spiritual powers of restraint and moderation. Fasting is not easy for everyone and should only be undertaken if one is physically fit and healthy and able to perform it without risking one's health or physical well-being. It involves abstaining from food and drink for a particular period of time. One could, for example, fast once a week, from sunrise to sunset. If one is unable to do this, one could fast once a month. Otherwise, one could set aside a particular week or weeks to fast in the year, as a sort of annual fast. This would be similar to the Qur'ānic practice of fasting during the lunar month of Ramadan. However one chooses to do it, fasting is a useful strategy to develop self-control and restraint. In Buddhism, monks practise fasting as part of their daily spiritual practices. They eat once a day, at one sitting, and reduce the amount that they eat. The practices are voluntary for lay practitioners of Buddhism.[258]

"There is no weapon so deadly as man's will. Excalibur is second to it."[259]

- Laozi

In Hinduism, there is a tradition that one should fast once a week from the beginning of the day until afternoon, although one is allowed to drink water during that time.[260] In the afternoon, one could have fruit juice and nuts and then break the fast after sunset.[261] Fasting is seen as a form of austerity, as it helps one to control one's senses, which helps one to develop God-consciousness. Srila Prabhupada argued that humans have four demands, viz. eating, sleeping, mating and defending. By letting these demands increase, many problems result. By decreasing these demands, our health can be improved and we develop temperance of habits.[262] In the Bhagavad-Gita, Krishna says: "Steadfast a lamp burns sheltered from the wind; such is the likeness of the Yogi's mind shut from sense-storms and burning bright to Heaven."[263] By restraining our physical appetites, we learn to control our bodies and our minds and free them from attachment to the lower self and our individuality.

Krishna says, furthermore, "The sovereign soul of him who lives self-governed and at peace is centred in itself, taking alike pleasure and pain; heat, cold; glory and shame."[264] In short:

- Fasting is a means for developing detachment and cleansing our hearts
- We should only practise fasting if we are physically able to
- We should fast at set times, such as once a week, once a month, or for a particular period of time each year
- There are different ways to fast, some allowing one to drink water and eat fruit
- Fasting is a mild form of austerity which allows us to limit our physical demands
- Fasting helps us to reach a stage of steadfastness and self-governance

"THIS world is a stage or market-place passed by pilgrims on their way to the next. It is here that they are to provide themselves with provisions for the way; or, to put it plainly, man acquires here, by the use of his bodily senses, some knowledge of the works of God, and, through them, of God Himself, the sight of whom will constitute his future beatitude. It

is for the acquirement of this knowledge that the spirit of man has descended into this world of water and clay."[265]

- Al-Ghazali, *The Alchemy of Happiness*, Chapter II

STEP 2 – RECOGNIZE THE ATTRIBUTES OF THE DIVINE IN ALL THINGS

The next step in cultivating a process of God-consciousness is to recognize the Divine in all things. This does not mean pantheism, or believing that all things are of one essence with God. That would be impossible, as all things are created by God and emanate from the Primal Will, the Primordial Word, which issues from the fathomless depths of eternity. Rather, it means recognizing that the entire world—the whole physical universe with all of its billions and trillions of galaxies and stars and, beyond it, all the dimensions and other universes that exist within the multi-verse (if such exists)—indeed, all of it is a mirror of the Divine. Each and every atom of existence manifests one or more of the attributes of God. Even in the smallest of elements—the atom—we see power, which is an attribute of God, the All-Powerful.

"There was a Door to which I found no Key:

There was a Veil past which I could not see:

Some little Talk awhile of ME and THEE

There seemed—and then no more of THEE and ME."[266]

- Omar Khayyam, *The Rubaiyat*, XXXII.

In the sun, we see the attribute of Light, which represents the Divine Light. In water, we see abundance, which is the attribute of magnanimity. In the tree, we see steadfastness. In the wind, we see transcendence. In the rock, we see permanence. In the axe, we see keenness. In the scalpel, we see precision. In the frog, we see patience. In the cat, we see grace. In the dog, we see loyalty. In the farmer, we see cultivation. In the banker, we see responsibility. In the king, we see justice. In the cleaner, we see cleanliness. In the executioner, we see wrath. In the lawyer, we see solicitude. In the physician, we see healing. In the mother, we see care and loving-kindness. In the father, we see determination. These are all examples rather than exact descriptions. However, they demonstrate a mind-set which sees the Divine in all things. In every human being, we see nobility, and in every face, we see the Face of God. In short:

- We should recognize the Divine in all things
- We should see the whole of creation as a mirror of the Divine
- We should recognize the essential Attributes of God which are manifest in all things
- In every person, we should see nobility and the Face of God

"When love of God kindles a flame in the inward man,

He burns, and is freed from effects.

He has no need of signs to assure him of Love,

For Love casts its own Light up to heaven."[267]

- Rumi, *The Masnavi*

STEP 3 – PRACTISE DHIKR, CHANTING HOLY WORDS AND VERSES

In Chapter 12, we mentioned mantra meditation, in which one sits (or walks) and repeats a mantra over and over again. This is a common practice in Sufism, which is the mystical element of Islam. Sufism focuses on the love between the individual and the Beloved, i.e. God. The Sufi practice of repetition is called *dhikr*, which means 'remembrance'. The 'dh' is pronounced like the 'th' in then. In Persian, however, it is pronounced *zekr*. In any case, it means mentioning God and remembering Him at all times. As God says in the Qur'ān: "And make mention of the name of thy Lord at morn, at even, and at night. Adore him, and praise him the livelong night."[268]

The Names of God are endless and innumerable, as they all reveal His divine Attributes and Qualities. Krishna says, for example, speaking in the Voice of God: "Whoever serve Me—as I show Myself—constantly true, in full devotion fixed, those hold I very holy. But who serve—worshipping Me, The One, The Invisible, The Unrevealed, Unnamed, Unthinkable, Uttermost, All-pervading, Highest, Sure—Who thus adore Me, mastering their sense, of one set mind to all, glad in all good, these blessed souls come unto Me."[269] Gautama Buddha, likewise, said: "There is, O monks, an unborn, unoriginated, uncreated, unformed. Were there not, O monks, this unborn, unoriginated, uncreated, unformed, there would be no escape from the world of the born, originated, created, formed."[270]

"Kindle in thy heart the flame of Love,
And burn up utterly thoughts and fine
expressions."[271]
- Rumi, *The Masnavi*

Likewise, in the Qur'ān, God says, glorified be He: "SAY: Call upon God (*Allāh*), or call upon the God of Mercy (*Arrahmān*), by whichsoever ye will invoke him: He hath most excellent names. And be not loud in thy prayer, neither pronounce it too low but between these follow a middle way."[272] In Islamic tradition, there are 99 Names of God and one Hidden Name, which will be revealed at the end of time. Likewise, in the Bible, there are numerous names for God. This website gives a list of 930 Names of God.[273] If we add those to the 99 traditional Arabic Names of God, then we have at least a 1,000 different Names, not including those mentioned in the Zoroastrian, Hindu and Buddhist scriptures. Zhuangzi refers to God as the 'Ultimate Cause'.[274]

The names of God are limitless, unbounded by the limits of human understanding. Nevertheless, by mentioning these Names and Attributes, we are evoking their inner power and reminding ourselves of them. We are drawing ourselves closer to the Divine, like moths absorbed with light, which get consumed by the fire and completely vanish. Even so, our egos and individuality should vanish in our all-consuming love for the Divine. By practicing *dhikr*, we practice remembrance of our true Creator and align ourselves with His Primal Will, which generates all created things and imbues them with the qualities of His Attributes.

"As the kindled flame
Feeds on the fuel till it sinks to ash,
So unto ash, Arjuna! unto nought
The flame of Knowledge wastes works'
dross away!"
- Krishna, *The Bhagavad-Gita*, Chapter IV

Practise reciting some of the Names of God throughout your day and constantly try to remember God. Write the Names of God in your notebook, use them on t-shirts or shirts. Draw them beautifully or print off a calligraphic representation of the Divine Names. Make them part of your everyday life. Use these as tools for remembering God. Combine this with prayers and meditation so that you can condition yourself to a higher level of thinking. In every aspect of your life, the Name of God should be present in your mind. In short:

- *Dhikr* (or *zekr*) means 'remembrance of God' through mentioning His Names
- God commands us to mention Him at morn, at even and at night
- There are many Names of God in all religions, including Hinduism and Buddhism
- There are 99 traditional Names of God in Islam and over 900 in the Bible
- We should mention these names in order to evoke their inner power
- We should be like moths consumed by love for the light, extinguishing our own egos in the fire of God's love
- We should practice reciting the Names of God, write them in our notebooks and read them

- We should combine this with the practices of prayer and meditation
- We can print off calligraphic representations of the Names of God, or draw them ourselves and post them on our walls to remind us of God at all times

"We have sent our apostles with the clear tokens, and we have caused the Book and the balance to descend with them, that men might observe fairness."[275]

- The Qur'ān 57:25

STEP 4 – STUDY THE LIVES OF THE PROPHETS & GREAT TEACHERS

We can only come to understand the Divine if we understand the lives of those Great Teachers who came into this world to provide Divine guidance, such as Abraham, Krishna, Moses, Buddha, Jesus and Muhammad. These are the Guides to the Eternal, the pure Mirrors of Truth who have brought the Light of God into the world through their teachings and their spiritual power, which radiates throughout all eternity, and the holy Words which they revealed, which resonate throughout all time. If we learn about their lives, we will come to love them, and if we love them with great and pure love, then we will also love God. By loving Abraham, we love God. By loving Moses, we love God. By loving Rama, we love God. By loving Krishna, we love God. By loving Buddha, we love God. By loving Zoroaster, we love God. By loving Jesus Christ, we love God. By loving Muhammad, we love God. These are Lamps of Divine Guidance and Wellsprings of Eternity. When we align our hearts with theirs and our faces to theirs, then we become channels for divine mercy, even as they are ultimate channels of divine mercy, power and grace.

There are many books available on the lives of these Great Teachers. The stories of many of the Judaeo-Christian Prophets can be found in the Bible. The Qur'ān, on the other hand, is not a biographical work or narrative, so it does not contain the life of the Prophet. For that, one must refer to a number of good biographies, such as those of Martin Lings (1983)[276] and Karen Armstrong (1992),[277] which are in English. There is also *Muhammad and the Course of Islam* by HM Balyuzi (1976) and *Muhammad at Mecca* and

Muhammad at Medina, both by W. Montgomery Watt (1953, 1956). Many biographies of the Prophet have been written throughout the centuries, however, both in the original Arabic and in other languages. Some of these are polemical, while others are scholarly, and yet others have an overreliance on miracles and miraculous events.

There are a number of good books about Gautama Buddha, such as *The God of Buddha* by Jamshed Fozdar (1973) (not a biography but still a very interesting book). Other books can be found on the lives of Zoroaster and Krishna. Krishna's story, though mixed with a lot of mythology and fantastical events, can be found in the *Srimad-Bhagavatam* and the *Mahabharata*, which are both available in English translations. A much shorter account of Krishna's life can be found in *Krsna, The Supreme Personality of Godhead*, by A.C. Bhaktivedanta Swami Prabhupada (1972). This latter book also includes a lot of the afore-mentioned mythology and miracles of Krishna. In short:

- We can only understand the Divine if we understand the Great Teachers

- These Teachers are Guides to the Eternal and pure Mirrors of Truth
- If we learn about their lives and come to love them, then we can truly love God
- When we align our hearts with theirs and turn our faces to them, then we become channels for divine mercy to flow from them to us
- We should read about the lives of some or all of these Teachers. There are many books available on most of them

"In the adorations and benedictions of righteous men

The praises of all the prophets are kneaded together.

All their praises are mingled into one stream,

All the vessels are emptied into one ewer.

Because He that is praised is, in fact, only One."[278]

- Rumi, *The Masnavi*

STEP 5 – EMBRACE THE TEACHINGS OF THE GREAT TEACHERS

The final step, which is the most important, is to embrace the Teachings of the Great Teachers. By that, we mean, embrace all of their Teachings as being true. That does not mean that one must follow the path of all the religions and obey all of their laws and commandments. That would be impossible for any man, as some of these are contradictory. At one time and place, it was ordained that wine was permissible. At another, it was forbidden. In one religion, divorce was permitted. In other, it was forbidden. The laws and commandments of religions differ over time and do not constitute the core of the religion. That is not to say that the laws and commandments are unimportant. They are. But we only need to follow the latest laws and commandments, rather than the ones of previous eons and ages, as the circumstances and conditions of life have changed immensely since those times. It is up to the individual to seek out the Truth for themselves and determine which laws and teachings one should follow. The basic moral teachings, however, are the same, as are the core of virtues, and the essential principles. This book has looked into many of them and found them accordant. Likewise, their teachings are in conformity with a number of Sages and Teachers who did not claim divinity and were ordinary men, like Laozi, Confucius, Plato, Aristotle and Epictetus, whose works we have quoted in this book.

What we need, as human beings, is guidance. And guidance can only come from those who know the Way—i.e. the Great Teachers. Even as we recognize the one Light which shines in all these glorious Lamps, so likewise should we embrace each one of them and adhere to their central teachings, which are one and the same. By loving these Great Teachers and, thereby, loving God, we can attain true tranquillity and happiness. We can truly live the life of the Sage. As Zhuangzi writes:

> **"The repose of the Sage is not what the world calls repose. His repose is the result of his mental attitude. All creation could not disturb his equilibrium: hence his repose... The mind of the Sage being in repose becomes the mirror of the universe, the speculum of all creation. Repose, tranquillity, stillness, inaction,—these were the levels of the universe, the ultimate perfection of TAO. Therefore wise rulers and Sages rest therein."[279]**

Let us, therefore, turn to these Sources of Guidance, embrace their teachings and follow the path of God. In short:

- We should embrace the Teachings of the Great Teachers and Messengers of God
- We should embrace all of their Teachings as being true
- We do not have to follow the commandments and laws of *every* religion
- The laws and commandments of previous ages are no longer suitable for the modern day
- The core teachings and virtues of all the Great Teachers, and their principles, are the same
- We can even find a lot of great inspiration from teachers who were ordinary human beings, such as Laozi, Confucius, Plato, Aristotle, Marcus Aurelius, Epictetus, Rumi, Hafez and others
- As human beings, we need guidance, which can only come from the Great Teachers
- By loving the Great Teachers, we are loving God
- By so doing, we can attain true tranquillity and happiness

Questions for Reflection:

The following are some questions that will help us to reflect on what we have learned in this chapter:

1. Why is fasting important? What is the purpose of fasting?
2. What does it mean to recognize the Divine in all things?
3. What is *dhikr* and how can we practise it?
4. Why should we study the lives of the Great Prophets and Teachers of the past?
5. Why should we embrace the teachings of these Great Teachers?

∞∞∞∞∞∞∞∞∞∞∞∞∞∞∞∞∞∞∞∞∞∞∞∞

A Note To My Readers:

Dear friends, dear readers!

Now that you have finished the last chapter of this book, I would urge you to reflect on the words of George Fox who, having experienced this state of enkindlement, wrote: "Now I was come up in spirit through the flaming sword, into the paradise of God. All things were new; and all the creation gave unto me another smell than before, beyond what words can utter. I knew nothing but pureness, and innocency, and righteousness."280 My hope for you is that you will all choose to follow this path, which is the Straight Path, the Middle Way, and put all of these steps and teachings into practice. If you do, great results will ensue. If you set your mind to it, you can achieve all your spiritual goals and attain a state of true equilibrium and tranquillity. Then we will see all things as new, and all things will smell another smell. We will be wrapped in purity and righteousness. Then we will be ready to live the true life, the life of the soul. This is the philosophy of balance—what I call the philosophy of equanimity. May God, who has created all things, bless each one of you and fill you with His

Light and Spirit. And peace be upon all the Messengers of God and the Prophets and their families and companions.

Don't forget to visit mwtumaini.org and check out the work that Msingi wa Tumaini is doing in Kenya. If you enjoyed reading this book and want to put the art of generous giving into practice, then please set up a monthly donation to Msingi wa Tumaini or give a one-off donation via Msingi wa Tumaini's JustGiving page, and make sure to follow Msingi wa Tumaini on Twitter: https://twitter.com/mwtumaini and Facebook: https://www.facebook.com/Msingi-wa-Tumaini-274916052612441/?fref=ts. Also, please check out my blog, Equanimity Blog (https://fivewaystobe.wordpress.com/), for a list of other recommended charities: https://fivewaystobe.wordpress.com/2017/02/06/recommended-charities-charitable-organizations/ Also be sure to follow Equanimity Blog on Twitter @https://twitter.com/equanimityblog/. You can also follow the author @https://twitter.com/Nicholas19.

Please do not forget to leave an honest review on Amazon, whether you liked the book or not, and share this book with your friends and family, so that they may also benefit therefrom.

BEFORE YOU GO, DON'T FORGET TO GET YOUR FREE GIVEAWAY! CLICK HERE (https://forms.aweber.com/form/98/1296528998.htm) TO SIGN UP TO RECEIVE YOUR FREE BONUS: A PDF FILE OF MORE INSPIRATIONAL QUOTATIONS! THESE ARE YET MORE QUOTATIONS WHICH CAN HELP TO INSPIRE YOU ON A DAILY BASIS!

∞∞∞∞∞∞∞∞∞∞∞∞∞∞∞∞∞∞∞∞∞∞∞∞

Check Out My Other Book

Below you'll find my other currently-published book on Amazon and Kindle, called *Green Monk of Tremn, Book I*. Simply click on the link below to check it out. Alternatively, you can visit my author page on Amazon to see other works I have written.

Green Monk of Tremn, Book I: An Epic Journey of Mystery and Adventure:
https://www.amazon.com/Green-Monk-Tremn-Book-Adventure-ebook/dp/B01NAYSPA8/

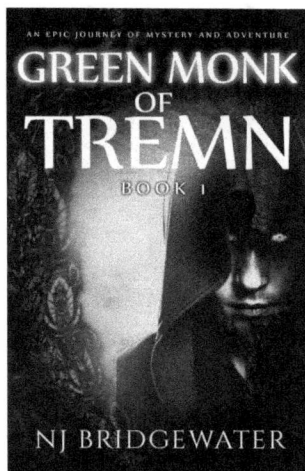

Green Monk of Tremn is the story of Ifunka Kaffa, a green-skinned alien boy from the planet Tremn who was abandoned by his mother and raised by his uncle and aunt, only to see them slaughtered at the hands of vicious assassins. This is the story of how Ifunka becomes a monk, facing unimaginable trials and ordeals. One day, his friend goes missing and he sets out with two other companions on an epic journey of adventure, mystery and intrigue. The three boys battle with their emotions, discover new truths and fight against terrible monsters and evil forces. It is a journey through the darkest of woods and hidden cities, through ancient kingdoms and lost valleys. It is a journey which you will never forget!

If the link does not work, for whatever reason, you can simply search for the title on the Amazon website to find it.

Bibliography

Philosophy

Abū Hāmid Muhammad ibn Muhammad Al-Ghazālī (author), Claud Field (translator) *The Alchemy of Happiness by Al Ghazzali, Translated from the Hindustani* (London: John Murray, Albermarle Street). Available online at: https://en.wikisource.org/wiki/The_Alchemy_of_Happiness_(Field) (accessed 14/12/2016)

Aristotle (author) F.H. Peters (translator) (1893) *The Nicomachean Ethics of Aristotle* (London: C. Kegan Paul). Available online at: http://oll.libertyfund.org/titles/aristotle-the-nicomachean-ethics (accessed 15/12/2016)

Averroes (Ibn Rushd) (author), Mohammad Jamil-Ub-Behman Barod (1921) *The Philosophy and Theology of Averroes* (Baroda: Manibhai Mathurbhal Gupta). Available online at: http://oll.libertyfund.org/titles/rushd-the-philosophy-and-theology-of-averroes (accessed 14/12/2016)

Sir Francis Bacon, Joseph Devey (editor) (1901) *The Advancement of Learning* (New York: P.F. Collier and Son). Available online at: http://oll.libertyfund.org/titles/bacon-the-advancement-of-learning (accessed 14/12/2016)

Paul Bunyan (1853) *The Pilgrim's Progress From This World to That Which is to Come; Delivered under the Similitude of a Dream* (Auburn: Derby & Miller, Buffalo: Geo. H. Derby and Co.). Available online at: https://www.ccel.org/ccel/bunyan/pilgrim.i.html (accessed 04/01/2017)

Marcus Tullius Cicero (author), Andrew P. Peabody (translator) (1887) *Ethical Writings of Cicero: De Oficiis; De Senectute; De Amicitia, and Scipio's Dream* (Boston: Little, Brown, and Co.). Available online at: http://oll.libertyfund.org/titles/cicero-on-moral-duties-de-officiis (accessed 14/12/2016)

Confucius (author), James Legge (translator) (1861) *The Chinese Classics — Volume 1: Confucian Analects* (London: Trübner). Available online at: http://www.gutenberg.org/ebooks/4094 (accessed 14/12/2016)

Marcus Aurelius Antoninus Augustus (author), George Long (translator) (1890) *The thoughts of the Emperor Marcus Aurelius Antoninus* (Boston: Litle, Brown). Available online at: http://classics.mit.edu/Antoninus/meditations.html (accessed 14/12/2016)

Epictetus (author), P.E. Matheson (translator) (1916) *Epictetus, The Discourses and Manual, together with fragments of his writings* (Oxford: Clarendon Press). Available online at: http://www.sacred-texts.com/cla/dep/index.htm (accessed 22/12/2016)

Lao-Tse (Laozi) (author), James Legge (translator) (1891) *The Tâo Teh King, or The Tao and Its Characteristics* (Oxford: Clarendon Press). Available online at: http://www.gutenberg.org/ebooks/216 (accessed 14/12/2016)

Plato (author), Benjamin Jowett (translator) (1888) *The Republic of Plato* (Oxford: Clarendon Press). Available online at: http://www.gutenberg.org/ebooks/1497 (accessed 15/12/2016)

Zhuangzi (author), Herbert Allen Giles (translator) (1889) *Chuang Tzu, Mystic, Moralist, and Social Reformer* (London: B. Quaritch). Available online at: https://archive.org/details/chuangtzumysticm00chu a (accessed 31/12/2016)

Poetry

Abū Hamīd ibn Abū Bakr Ibrāhīm ('Attār of Nishapur) (author), Edward Fitzgerald (translator) (1889) Bird Parliament. In Edward Fitzgerald (1889) *Letters and literary remains* (London: Macmillan). Available online at: http://www.sacred-texts.com/isl/bp/bp01.htm (accessed 14/12/2016)

F. Hadland Davis (1920) *Jalálu'd-Dín Rúmí* (London: John Murray). Available online at: http://www.gutenberg.org/ebooks/45159 (accessed 15/12/2016)

Ghiyāthu'd-Dīn Abu'l-Fath 'Umar ibn Ibrāhīm Nīshāpūrī (Omar Khayyām) (author), Edward Fitzgerald (translator) (1881) *Rubaíyát of Omar Khayyam: the astronomer-poet of Persia* (Boston: Houghton, Mifflin; Cambridge: Riverside Press). Available online at:

http://www.gutenberg.org/ebooks/246 (accessed 15/12/2016)

Khwāja Shamsu'd-Dīn Muhammad (Hafez of Shiraz) (author), Gertrude Lowthian Bell (translator) (1897) *Poems from the Divan of Hafiz* (London: Heinemann). Available online at: http://sacred-texts.com/isl/pdh/index.htm (accessed 19/12/2016)

Khwāja Shamsu'd-Dīn Muhammad (Hafez of Shiraz) (author), Elizabeth Bridges (author) (1921) *Sonnets from Hafez & other verses* (Oxford: Oxford University Press). Available online at: http://www.gutenberg.org/ebooks/49716 (accessed 15/12/2016)

Jalālu'd-Dīn Rūmī (author), E.H. Whinfield (translator) (1898) *Masnavi i Ma'navi, The Spiritual Couplets of Maulana Jalálu-'d-Dín Muhammad i Rúmí* (London: Trübner & Co.). Available online at: http://www.sacred-texts.com/isl/masnavi/index.htm ; https://archive.org/details/cu31924026910251 (accessed 22/12/2016).

Jalālu'd-Dīn Rūmī (author), Reynold Alleyne Nicholson (translator) (1926) *The Mathnawí of Jalálu'ddín Rúmí* (Havertown: Gibb Memorial Trust).

Available online at:
http://www.worldprayerfoundation.com/Rumi-Books%201%20and%202.pdf (accessed 15/12/2016)

Abū-Muhammad Muslihu'd-Dīn 'Abdu'llāh Shīrāzī (Saadi) (author), A. Hart Edwards (translator) (1911) *The Bustān of Sadi* (London: John Murray), Chapter II, p. 48. Available online at: http://www.sacred-texts.com/isl/bus/index.htm (24/12/2016)

Abū-Muhammad Muslihu'd-Dīn 'Abdu'llāh Shīrāzī (Saadi) (author), Richard J. H. Gottheil (translator) (1900) *Persian Literature comprising the Sháh Námeh, the Rubáiyát, the Divan, and the Gulistan.* Revised Edition, Volume 2. (New York: Collier) Available online at: http://www.gutenberg.org/ebooks/13060 (accessed 15/12/2016)

Abū-Muhammad Muslihu'd-Dīn 'Abdu'llāh Shīrāzī (Saadi) (author), Arthur N. Wollaston (translator) (1906) *Sadi's Scroll of Wisdom* (London: J. Murray). Available online at: http://www.sacred-texts.com/isl/ssw/ssw00.htm (accessed 24/12/2016)

Hakîm Abû'l-Majd Majdûd Sanâ'î of Ghazna (author), J. Stephenson (translator) (1910) *The First Book of the Hadîqatu'l-Haqîqat or, The Enclosed Garden of the Truth* (Calcutta: Asiatic Society). Available online at: http://www.sacred-texts.com/isl/egt/index.htm (accessed 22/12/2016)

Religion and Spirituality

St. Thomas Aquinas (author), The Very Rev. Hugh Pope (translator) (1914) *On Prayer and the Contemplative Life* (London: R. & T. Washbourne). Available online at: http://www.gutenberg.org/ebooks/22295 (accessed 14/12/2016)

Siddhartha Gautama Buddha (author), W.D.C. Wagiswara & K.J. Saunders (translators) (1920) *The Buddha's Way of Virtue, A Translation from the Dhammapada from the Pali Text* (London: John Murray). Available online at: http://www.sacred-texts.com/bud/wov/index.htm (accessed 21/12/2016)

Siddhartha Gautama Buddha (author), Henry Clarke Warren (translator) (1896) *Buddhism in translations: passages selected from the Buddhist sacred books and translated from the original Pali*

240

into English (Cambridge, Mass.: Harvard University Press). Available online at: http://sacred-texts.com/bud/bits/index.htm (accessed 21/12/2016).

Siddhartha Gautama Buddha (author), T.W. Rhys Davids (translator) (1899) *Dialogues of the Buddha {The Dîgha-Nikâya}, Translated from the Pâli* (London: Oxford University Press). Available online at: http://www.sacred-texts.com/bud/dob/index.htm (accessed 21/12/2016).

Siddhartha Gautama Buddha (author), Max Müller (translator) (1881) *The Dhammapada, a Collection of Verses; being one of the canonical books of the Buddhists* (Oxford: The Clarendon Press). Available online at: http://www.sacred-texts.com/bud/sbe10/index.htm (accessed 14/12/2016)

Siddhartha Gautama Buddha (author), W.H.D. Rouse (translator), E.B. Cowell (editor) (1895) *The Jātaka, or Stories of the Buddha's Former Births, translated from the Pāli by various hands, Vol. II* (Cambridge: Cambridge University Press). Available online at: http://www.sacred-texts.com/bud/j2/index.htm (accessed 21/12/2016).

Siddhartha Gautama Buddha (author), Viggo Fausböll (translator) (1881) *The Sutta-Nipâta, Translated by the Pâli.* In Vol. IX of *The Sacred Books of the East* (Oxford: The Clarendon Press). Available online at: http://www.sacred-texts.com/bud/sbe10/ (accessed 04/01/2017)

Paul Carus (1894) *Buddha, The Gospel* (Chicago: The Open Court Publishing Company). Available online at: http://www.sacred-texts.com/bud/btg/index.htm (accessed 28/01/2017).

Paul Carus (author), Olga Kopetzky (illustrator) (1915) *The Gospel of Buddha, Compiled from Ancient Records* (Chicago; London: The Open Court Publishing Company). Available online at: http://www.gutenberg.org/ebooks/35895 (accessed 16/11/2016)

George Fox (author), Rufus M. Jones (editor) (1906) *George Fox: An Autobiography* (Philadelphia: Ferris & Leach). Available online at: http://www.strecorsoc.org/gfox/title.html (accessed 15/12/2016)

Thomas à Kempis (author), William Benham (translator) (1886) *The Imitation of Christ* (London:

J.C. Nimmo). Available online at: http://www.sacred-texts.com/chr/ioc/index.htm (accessed 25/12/2016)

The King James Version (KJV) (1611), also known as the Authorized Version (AV), or the King James Bible (KJB). URL: http://www.gutenberg.org/ebooks/10 (accessed 20/12/2016)

Kaiten Nukariya (1913) *The Religion of the Samurai, A Study of Zen Philosophy and Discipline in China and Japan* (Auckland: Floating Press). Available online at: http://www.sacred-texts.com/bud/rosa/index.htm (accessed 26/12/2016)

Yejitsu Okusa (1915) *Principal Teachings of The True Sect of Pure Land* (Kyōto: The Ōtaniha Hongwanji),. Available online at: http://www.sacred-texts.com/bud/ptpl/index.htm (accessed 30/12/2016)

E.H. Palmer (1880) *The Qur'ân, Part II*. In E.H. Palmer (1880) *The Sacred Books of the East, Vol. 9* (Oxford: At the Clarendon Press). Available online at: http://www.sacred-texts.com/isl/sbe09/index.htm (accessed 22/12/2016)

Swami Paramananda (1919) *The Upanishads, Translated and Commentated by Swami Paramananda, From the Original Sanskrit Text* (Boston: Vedanta Centre). Available online at: http://www.gutenberg.org/ebooks/3283 (accessed 20/12/2016)

J. M. Rodwell (1876) *El-Kor'ân, or, The Koran* (London: B. Quaritch). URL: http://www.sacred-texts.com/isl/qr/index.htm; http://www.gutenberg.org/ebooks/3434 (accessed 17/12/2016)

R.F St. Andrew St. John (translator) (1893) Kumbha Jâtaka or the Hermit Varu.na Sûra and the Hunter (Jâtaka 512), *Journal of the Royal Asiatic Society* (London: The Royal Asiatic Society). Available online at: http://www.sacred-texts.com/journals/jras/1893-14.htm (accessed 28/01/2017)

Veda-Vyāsa (author), Kisari Mohan Gangulia (translator) (1919) *The Mahabharata of Krishna-Dwaipayana Vyasa*, Book 12 (Part one of three): Santi Parva. Translated into English Prose from the Original Sanskrit Text (Calcutta: D. Bose & Co.).

Available online at: http://www.sacred-texts.com/hin/m12/index.htm (accessed 30/12/2016)

Veda-Vyāsa (author), Sir Edwin Arnold (translator) (1900) *The Song Celestial; Or, Bhagavad-Gîtâ (from the Mahâbhârata): Being a Discourse Between Arjuna, Prince of India, and the Supreme Being, Under the Form of Krishna* (New York: Truslove, Hanson & Comba, Ltd.). Available online at: http://www.gutenberg.org/ebooks/2388 (accessed 16/11/2016)

W.D.C. Wagiswara, K.J. Saunders (translators) (1920) *The Buddha's "Way of Virtue": A Translation of the Dhammapada from the Pali Text* (London: John Murray). Available online at: http://www.sacred-texts.com/bud/wov/index.htm (accessed 28/01/2017)

John Wesley (1846) *Sermons on Several Occasions, Vol. III* (London: J. Mason). Available online at: https://archive.org/details/ra613718503wesluoft (accessed 22/12/2016).

Zoroaster (author), L. H. Mills (translator) (1898) *The Avesta: Yasna*. In L.H. Mills, James Darmesteter

(1898) *The Zend-Avesta, Parts I-III.* (New York: Christian Literature Co.). Available online at: http://www.sacred-texts.com/zor/sbe31/yasnae.htm (accessed 17/12/2016)

Other

S.G. Goodrich (1843) *Famous Men of Ancient Times* (Boston: Thompson, Brown & Company). Available online at: http://www.gutenberg.org/ebooks/52400 (accessed 17/12/2016)

John Wortabet (1913) *Arabian Wisdom* (London: J. Murray). Available online at: http://sacred-texts.com/isl/arw/index.htm (accessed 04/01/2017)

References:

[1] Siddharta Gautama Buddha (author), Viggo Fausböll (translator) (1881) *The Sutta-Nipâta, Translated from the Pâli*, I. Uragavagga, 1. Uragasutta, v. 181, p. 30.

[2] Siddharta Gautama Buddha (author), Max Müller (translator) (1881) *The Dhammapada, a Collection of Verses; being one of the canonical books of the Buddhists*, Chapter VI, v. 80.

[3] Plato (author), Benjamin Jowett (translator) (1888) *The Republic of Plato*, Book X.

[4] Benjamin Franklin (1750) *Poor Richard's Almanac*. Quoted in David Dunning, Chip Heath, Jerry Suls (2005) 'Know Thyself' — Easier Said Than Done, News Release, October 28, 2005. *Association for Psychological Science (APS)*. Available online at: http://www.psychologicalscience.org/media/releases/2005/pro 51028.cfm (accessed 15/12/2016).

[5] Lao-Tse (Laozi) (author), James Legge (translator) (1891) *The Tâo The King, or The Tao and Its Characteristics*, 33.1.

[6] Confucius (author), James Legge (translator) (1861) *The Chinese Classics — Volume 1: Confucian Analects*, Chapter V, 4.

[7] Attributed to Solomon, *The Book of Proverbs*. In the *Authorised Version* (or *King James Version* of the Bible). Available online at: https://www.biblegateway.com/passage/?search=Proverbs+1&version=KJV (accessed 15/12/2016).

[8] Confucius, *Confucian Analects*, Chapter XLV.

[9] Confucius, *Confucian Analects*, Chapter XX.

[10] See: S.G. Goodrich (1843) *Famous Men of Ancient Times* (Boston: Thompson, Brown & Company), p. 214. Available online at: http://www.gutenberg.org/ebooks/52400 (accessed 17/12/2016).

[11] See: Diogenes Laërtius (author), Robert Drew Hicks (translator) (1925) *Lives of the Eminent Philosophers* (New York: G.P. Putnam's Sons), Book VI. Available online at: https://en.wikisource.org/wiki/Lives_of_the_Eminent_Philosophers (accessed 17/12/2016).

[12] Siddharta Gautama Buddha (author), Max Müller (translator) (1881) *The Dhammapada, a Collection of Verses; being one of the canonical books of the Buddhists*, Ch. XVII., v. 221, p. 58.

[13] Confucius (author), James Legge (translator) (1861) *The Chinese Classics — Volume 1: Confucian Analects*, Book VII, Chapter XXIX.

[14] See: Paul Carus (author), Olga Kopetzky (illustrator) (1915) *The Gospel of Buddha, Compiled from Ancient Records*, pp. 7 – 10.

[15] Carus, pp. 13 – 14.

[16] Carus, pp. 14 – 15.

[17] Carus, p. 15.

[18] Carus, p. 15.

[19] Carus, pp. 18 – 42.

[20] Plato (author), Benjamin Jowett (translator) (1888) *The Republic of Plato*, Book X.

[21] Plato, *The Republic*, Book X.

[22] Ghiyāthu'd-Dīn Abu'l-Fath 'Umar ibn Ibrāhīm Nīshāpūrī (Omar Khayyām) (author), Edward Fitzgerald (translator) (1881) *Rubaíyát of Omar Khayyam: the astronomer-poet of Persia*, XII.

[23] Marcus Aurelius Antoninus Augustus (author), George Long (translator) (1890) *The thoughts of the Emperor Marcus Aurelius Antoninus*, Book II.

[24] Siddharta Gautama Buddha (author), Max Müller (translator) (1881) *The Dhammapada, a Collection of Verses; being one of the canonical books of the Buddhists*, Ch. 1, v. 18, p. 7.

[25] Buddha, The Dhammapada, Ch. IX., v. 118, p. 34.

[26] J. M. Rodwell (1876) *El-Kor'ân, or, The Koran*, 5:35.

[27] Marcus Aurelius Antoninus Augustus (author), George Long (translator) (1890) *The thoughts of the Emperor Marcus Aurelius Antoninus*, Book V.

28 Siddharta Gautama Buddha (author), Max Müller (translator) (1881) *The Dhammapada, a Collection of Verses; being one of the canonical books of the Buddhists*, Ch. XX, v. 274.

29 Paul Carus (author), Olga Kopetzky (illustrator) (1915) *The Gospel of Buddha, Compiled from Ancient Records*, p. 40.

30 Carus, p. 125.

31 Book of Proverbs 4:7. From the *King James Version (KJV)* of the Bible.

32 Matthew 7:24 – 27 (KJV).

33 Buddha, *The Dhammapada*, Ch. III, v. 35 – 36, p. 12.

34 Buddha, *The Dhammapada*, Ch. X, v. 133, p. 37.

35 Zoroaster (author), L. H. Mills (translator) (1898) *The Avesta: Yasna*. In L.H. Mills, James Darmesteter (1898) *The Zend-Avesta, Parts I-III*, Yasna – Introduction, v. 4.

36 St. Thomas Aquinas (author), The Very Rev. Hugh Pope (translator) (1914) *On Prayer and the Contemplative Life*, Question LXXXI, II, p. 34.

37 Buddha (author), W.D.C. Wagiswara, K.J. Saunders (translators) (1920) *The Buddha's Way of Virtue*, § XXIV, v. 339, p. 73.

38 Paul Carus (1894) *Buddha, The Gospel* (Chicago: The Open Court Publishing Company), Avoiding the Ten Evils.

39 Buddha, *The Dhammapada*, Ch. XIII, v. 173, p. 47

[40] Confucius (author), James Legge (translator) (1861) *The Chinese Classics — Volume 1: Confucian Analects*, Book IV, Ch. III.

[41] Marcus Aurelius Antoninus Augustus (author), George Long (translator) (1890) *The thoughts of the Emperor Marcus Aurelius Antoninus*, Book VI.

[42] J. M. Rodwell (1876) *El-Kor'ân, or, The Koran*, 18:46.

[43] Veda-Vyāsa (author), Sir Edwin Arnold (translator) (1900) *The Song Celestial; Or, Bhagavad-Gîtâ (from the Mahâbhârata): Being a Discourse Between Arjuna, Prince of India, and the Supreme Being, Under the Form of Krishna*, Ch. XVI.

[44] Siddharta Gautama Buddha (author), T.W. Rhys Davids (translator) (1899) *Dialogues of the Buddha {The Dîgha-Nikâya}, Translated from the Pâli* (London: Oxford University Press), II. Sâmañña-Phala Sutta [The Fruits of the Life of a Recluse], v. 65, pp. 80 – 81. Available online at: http://www.sacred-texts.com/bud/dob/index.htm (accessed 21/12/2016).

[45] Krishna, *The Bhagavad-Gita*, Ch. XV.

[46] Jalālu'd-Dīn Rūmī (author), Reynold Alleyne Nicholson (translator) (1926) *The Mathnawí of Jalálu'ddín Rúmí*, From Dīvān Shams-i-Tabrīz.

[47] Buddha, *The Dhammapada*, Ch. II, v. 23, p. 9.

[48] Krishna, *The Bhagavad-Gita*, Ch. VII.

49 Siddhartha Gautama Buddha (author), Max Müller (translator) (1881) *The Dhammapada, a Collection of Verses; being one of the canonical books of the Buddhists*, Ch. XIII, v. 170, p. 47.

50 Buddha, *The Dhammapada*, Chapter I, v. 2, p. 4.

51 Confucius (author), James Legge (translator) (1861) *The Chinese Classics — Volume 1: Confucian Analects*, Book XII, Ch. III, v. 2.

52 Averroes (Ibn Rushd) (author), Mohammad Jamil-Ub-Behman Barod (1921) *The Philosophy and Theology of Averroes*, I.

53 R.F St. Andrew St. John (translator) (1893) Kumbha Jâtaka or the Hermit Varu.na Sûra and the Hunter (Jâtaka 512), *Journal of the Royal Asiatic Society* (London: The Royal Asiatic Society), p. 569.

54 Buddha (author), F. Max Müller (translator) (1881) *The Dhammapada*, Chapter XVIII, p. 61.

55 Confucius, *Analects*, Book IV, Ch. IV.

56 Buddha (author), W.H.D. Rouse (translator), E.B. Cowell (editor) (1895) *The Jātaka, or Stories of the Buddha's Former Births, translated from the Pāli by various hands, Vol. II* (Cambridge: Cambridge University Press), No. 179. Stadhamma-Jātaka, p. 58. Available online at: http://www.sacred-texts.com/bud/j2/index.htm (accessed 21/12/2016).

57 See: Barbara O'Brien (2016) Right Livelihood: The Ethics of Earning a Living. Updated October 13, 2016. *About Religion*.

Available online at:
http://buddhism.about.com/od/theeightfoldpath/a/rightliveliho
od.htm (accessed 21/12/2016).

58 Siddharta Gautama Buddha (author), T.W. Rhys Davids
(translator) (1899) *Dialogues of the Buddha {The Dîgha-
Nikâya}, Translated from the Pâli* (London: Oxford University
Press), I. Brahma-Gâla Sutta [The Perfect Net], v. 21, pp. 17 – 19.

59 Siddhartha Gautama Buddha (author), W.D.C. Wagiswara
& K.J. Saunders (translators) (1920) *The Buddha's Way of
Virtue, A Translation from the Dhammapada from the Pali Text*
(London: John Murray). Available online at: http://www.sacred-
texts.com/bud/wov/index.htm (accessed 21/12/2016).

60 See: Barbara O'Brien (2015) Right Effort: Part of the
Eightfold Path. Updated December 09, 2015. *About Religion.*
Available online at:
http://buddhism.about.com/od/theeightfoldpath/a/Right-
Effort.htm (accessed 21/12/2016).

61 Veda-Vyāsa (author), Sir Edwin Arnold (translator)
(1900) *The Song Celestial; Or, Bhagavad-Gîtâ (from the
Mahâbhârata): Being a Discourse Between Arjuna, Prince of
India, and the Supreme Being, Under the Form of Krishna,*
Chapter VI.

62 Buddha (author), Henry Clarke Warren (translator)
(1896) *Buddhism in translations: passages selected from the
Buddhist sacred books and translated from the original Pa□li
into English* (Cambridge, Mass.: Harvard University Press),
Chapter IV. Meditation and Nirvana, § 74. Mahâ-Satipatthāna-
Sutta (The Four Intent Contemplations), pp. 357 – 358. Available

online at: http://sacred-texts.com/bud/bits/index.htm (accessed 21/12/2016).

63 Krishna, *The Bhagavad-Gita*, Ch. V.

64 Krishna, *The Bhagavad-Gita*, Ch. VI.

65 Abū-Muhammad Muslihu'd-Dīn 'Abdu'llāh Shīrāzī (Saadi) (author), Richard J. H. Gottheil (translator) (1900) *Persian Literature comprising the Shāh Nāmeh, the Rubáiyát, the Divan, and the Gulistan*, CH II, XII.

66 Paul Carus (author), Olga Kopetzky (illustrator) (1915) *The Gospel of Buddha, Compiled from Ancient Records*, XXVI., p. 81

67 Lao-Tse (Laozi) (author), James Legge (translator) (1891) *The Tâo Teh King, or The Tao and Its Characteristics*, Part I, 32.5.

68 Lao-Tse, *The Tâo Teh King*, Part I, 10.3.

69 Lao-Tse, *The Tâo Teh King*, Part II, 51.1.

70 Plato (author), Benjamin Jowett (translator) (1888) *The Republic of Plato*, Book II.

71 Siddhartha Gautama Buddha (author), Max Müller (translator) (1881) *The Dhammapada, a Collection of Verses; being one of the canonical books of the Buddhists*, Chapter XXIII – The Elephant, v. 320 – 324, p. 77.

72 Matthew 5:43 – 45 (King James Bible).

73 Abū Hāmid Muhammad ibn Muhammad Al-Ghazālī (author), Claud Field (translator) *The Alchemy of Happiness by Al Ghazzali, Translated from the Hindustani*, Chapter I.

[74] Veda-Vyāsa (author), Sir Edwin Arnold (translator) (1900) *The Song Celestial; Or, Bhagavad-Gîtâ (from the Mahâbhârata): Being a Discourse Between Arjuna, Prince of India, and the Supreme Being, Under the Form of Krishna,* Chapter IV.

[75] Veda-Vyāsa (author), Sir Edwin Arnold (translator) (1900) *The Song Celestial; Or, Bhagavad-Gîtâ (from the Mahâbhârata): Being a Discourse Between Arjuna, Prince of India, and the Supreme Being, Under the Form of Krishna,* Ch. XIII.

[76] St. Thomas Aquinas (author), The Very Rev. Hugh Pope (translator) (1914) *On Prayer and the Contemplative Life,* Question LXXXIII. On Prayer.

[77] In the original translation, the term is Ahura Mazdā. However, as this implies to the English reader that Ahura Mazdā is a particular Deity, rather than the one Creator of all, I have decided to render the name in English as Lord All-Wise or All-Wise Lord, as this is the literal meaning of Ahura Mazdā. Ahura refers to a divine being or lord, while mazdā refers to 'wisdom' or 'wise', which is also a title of God in the Qur'ān.

[78] Zoroaster (author), L.H. Mills (translator) (1898), in Mills (1898) *Sacred Books of the East,* 31 (Oxford: Oxford University Press), Yasna Haptanghaiti, 41.1-2. Available online at: http://www.avesta.org/yasna/yasna.htm (accessed 22/12/2016).

[79] *The Bhagavad-Gita,* Chapter XI.

[80] Jalālu'd-Dīn Rūmī (author), E.H. Whinfield (translator) (1898) *Masnavi i Ma'navi, The Spiritual Couplets of Maulana*

Jalálu-'d-Dín Muhammad i Rúmí (London: Trübner & Co.), Book II, Story X. Available online at: http://www.sacred-texts.com/isl/masnavi/index.htm ; https://archive.org/details/cu31924026910251 (accessed 22/12/2016).

[81] Siddhartha Gautama Buddha (author), Max Müller (translator) (1881) *The Dhammapada, a Collection of Verses; being one of the canonical books of the Buddhists,* Chapter XVIII., v. 241, p. 60.

[82] E.H. Palmer (1880) *The Qur'ân, Part II*, XX. The Chapter of T.H., v. 12 – 14, p. 35. In E.H. Palmer (1880) *The Sacred Books of the East, Vol. 9* (Oxford: At the Clarendon Press). Available online at: http://www.sacred-texts.com/isl/sbe09/index.htm (accessed 22/12/2016).

[83] In Rodwell's translation, we read: "Verily, I am thy Lord: therefore pull off thy shoes: for thou art in the holy valley of Towa. And I have chosen thee: hearken then to what shall be revealed. Verily, I am God: there is no God but me: therefore worship me, and observe prayer for a remembrance of me." J. M. Rodwell (1876) *El-Kor'ân, or, The Koran*, 20:12 – 14.

[84] The Rev. John Wesley (1846) *Sermons on Several Occasions, Vol. III* (London: J. Mason), Sermon XCVIII. On Visiting the Sick, par. 5, p. 117. Available online at: https://archive.org/details/ra613718503wesluoft (accessed 22/12/2016).

[85] Epictetus (author), P.E. Matheson (translator) (1916) *Epictetus, The Discourses and Manual, together with fragments of his writings* (Oxford: Clarendon Press), Chapter XI. On

Cleanliness, p. 450. Available online at: http://www.sacred-texts.com/cla/dep/index.htm (accessed 22/12/2016).

86 Hakîm Abû'l-Majd Majdûd Sanâ'î of Ghazna (author), J. Stephenson (translator) (1910) *The First Book of the Hadîqatu'l-Haqîqat or, The Enclosed Garden of the Truth* (Calcutta: Asiatic Society), On the Participation of the Heart in Prayer, pp. 116 – 117. Available online at: http://www.sacred-texts.com/isl/egt/index.htm (accessed 22/12/2016).

87 Sanâ'î of Ghazna, *The First Book of the Hadîqatu'l-Haqîqat or, The Enclosed Garden of the Truth*, p. 47.

88 Sanâ'î of Ghazna, *The First Book of the Hadîqatu'l-Haqîqat or, The Enclosed Garden of the Truth*, p. 81.

89 2 Corinthians 5:18 (King James Bible).

90 Qur'ān 10:56 (Rodwell translation).

91 Qur'ān 8:61 (Rodwell translation).

92 Veda-Vyāsa (author), Sir Edwin Arnold (translator) (1900) *The Song Celestial; Or, Bhagavad-Gîtâ*, Chapter V.

93 Jalālu'd-Dīn Rūmī (author), E.H. Whinfield (translator) (1898) *Masnavi i Ma'navi, The Spiritual Couplets of Maulana Jalálu-'d-Dín Muhammad i Rúmí*, Book III, Story XI. Bahlol and the Darvesh.

94 Qur'ān 20:130 (Rodwell translation).

95 St. Thomas Aquinas (author), The Very Rev. Hugh Pope (translator) (1914) *On Prayer and the Contemplative Life*, Question LXXXIII, II, p. 75.

[96] St. Thomas Aquinas, *On Prayer and the Contemplative Life*, Question LXXXIII, II, p. 75.

[97] Proverbs 3:3 (King James Bible).

[98] Quoted in St. Thomas Aquinas, *On Prayer and the Contemplative Life*, Question CLXXX, VI, p. 92.

[99] Jalālu'd-Dīn Rūmī (author), E.H. Whinfield (translator) (1898) *Masnavi i Ma'navi, The Spiritual Couplets of Maulana Jalálu-'d-Dín Muhammad i Rúmí*, Book III, Story II.

[100] Qur'ān 2:186 (Rodwell translation).

[101] Qur'ān 55:78 (Rodwell translation).

[102] Qur'ān 76:25 (Rodwell translation).

[103] Qur'ān 8:61 (Rodwell translation).

[104] Qur'ān 35:21 (Rodwell translation).

[105] Proverbs 3:5 (King James Bible).

[106] Psalm 27:1 (King James Bible).

[107] Abū Hāmid Muhammad ibn Muhammad Al-Ghazālī (author), Claud Field (translator) *The Alchemy of Happiness by Al Ghazzali*, Chapter II.

[108] Buddha, *The Dhammapada*, Ch. IX., v. 118, p. 34.

[109] Proverb 3:3 (King James Bible).

[110] Buddha, *The Dhammapada*, Ch. XIII, v. 169, p. 47.

[111] Confucius (author), James Legge (translator) (1861) *The Chinese Classics — Volume 1: Confucian Analects*, Book XII, Ch. IV, v. 1.

[112] Veda-Vyāsa (author), Sir Edwin Arnold (translator) (1900) *The Song Celestial; Or, Bhagavad-Gîtâ (from the Mahâbhârata): Being a Discourse Between Arjuna, Prince of India, and the Supreme Being, Under the Form of Krishna*, Ch. XVIII.

[113] Krishna, *The Bhagavad-Gita*, Ch. XVIII.

[114] Marcus Aurelius Antoninus Augustus (author), George Long (translator) (1890) *The thoughts of the Emperor Marcus Aurelius Antoninus*, Book VII.

[115] Carown = Qārūn, a wealthy individual who became arrogant due to pride and ignorance. He was punished by God by being swallowed up into earth, along with all his material wealth. The story derives from that of Korah, son of Izhar, in the Book of Exodus.

[116] Nushirowan = Khosrow I (Chosroes I), also known as Anushiruwān the Just, King of Kings of Persia, who reigned from 531 to 579 CE. He was a ruler of the Sassanian Empire who was renowned for his justice, wisdom and generosity. He introduced a rational tax system and was interested in literature and philosophy.

[117] Abū-Muhammad Muslihu'd-Dīn 'Abdu'llāh Shīrāzī (Saadi) (author), Richard J. H. Gottheil (translator) (1900) *Persian Literature comprising the Sháh Námeh, the Rubáiyát, the Divan, and the Gulistan*, CH I, XVIII.

[118] Confucius (author), James Legge (translator) (1861) *The Chinese Classics — Volume 1: Confucian Analects*, Book XVII, Chapter VI.

[119] Luke 12:15 –21 (King James Bible).

[120] Abū-Muhammad Muslihu'd-Dīn 'Abdu'llāh Shīrāzī (Saadi) (author), Arthur N. Wollaston (translator) (1906) *Sadi's Scroll of Wisdom* (London: J. Murray). Available online at: http://www.sacred-texts.com/isl/ssw/ssw00.htm (accessed 24/12/2016).

[121] Romans 15:1 – 2 (King James Bible).

[122] Luke 10:25 (King James Bible).

[123] Luke 10:26 (King James Bible).

[124] Luke 10:27 (King James Bible).

[125] Luke 10:28 (King James Bible).

[126] Qur'ān 2:215 (Rodwell translation).

[127] Qur'ān 30:37 – 38 (Rodwell translation).

[128] Marcus Tullius Cicero (author), Andrew P. Peabody (translator) (1887) *Ethical Writings of Cicero: De Oficiis; De Senectute; De Amicitia, and Scipio's Dream*, Book 1.14.

[129] Aristotle (author) F.H. Peters (translator) (1893) *The Nicomachean Ethics of Aristotle*, Book IV, 1.

[130] Paul Carus (author), Olga Kopetzky (illustrator) (1915) *The Gospel of Buddha, Compiled from Ancient Records*, p. 74.

[131] 2 Corinthians 9:7 (King James Bible).

[132] 1 John 3:17 (King James Bible).

[133] Qur'ān 4:1 (Palmer translation).

[134] Qur'ān 49:13 (Rodwell translation).

135 Qur'ān 2:213 (Rodwell translation).

136 Qur'ān 4:36 (Rodwell translation).

137 Galatians 3:28 (King James Bible).

138 John 13:36 (King James Bible).

139 Luke 6:38 (King James Bible).

140 James 2:15 – 16 (King James Bible).

141 Proverbs 11:24 – 25 (King James Bible).

142 Qur'ān 16:90 (Rodwell translation).

143 Qur'ān 29:8 (Rodwell translation).

144 John Wortabet (1913) *Arabian Wisdom* (London: J. Murray), p. 23.

145 Abū-Muhammad Muslihu'd-Dīn 'Abdu'llāh Shīrāzī (Saadi) (author), A. Hart Edwards (translator) (1911) *The Bustān of Sadi* (London: John Murray), Chapter II, p. 48. Available online at: http://www.sacred-texts.com/isl/bus/index.htm (24/12/2016).

146 Paul Carus (author), Olga Kopetzky (illustrator) (1915) *The Gospel of Buddha, Compiled from Ancient Records*, LIV., pp. 160 – 163.

147 Carus (1915), p. 160.

148 The Editors of Encyclopædia Britannica (2016) Tathagata (article), *Encyclopædia Britannica*. Available online at: https://global.britannica.com/topic/Tathagata (accessed 25/12/2016).

[149] Siddhartha Gautama Buddha (author), Max Müller (translator) (1881) *The Dhammapada, a Collection of Verses; being one of the canonical books of the Buddhists*, Chapter XIV, v. 193 – 194, p. 52.

[150] Buddha, *The Dhammapada*, Ch. XIV, v. 190 – 192.

[151] F. Hadland Davis (1920) *Jalálu'd-Dín Rúmí*, p. 102.

[152] Qur'ān 51:20 – 23 (Rodwell translation).

[153] Qur'ān 39:27 (Rodwell translation).

[154] Qur'ān 18:32 – 35 (Rodwell translation).

[155] Qur'ān 18:36 (Rodwell translation).

[156] Qur'ān 18:37 – 41 (Rodwell translation).

[157] Qur'ān 18:42 - 44 (Rodwell translation).

[158] Qur'ān 18:45 (Rodwell translation).

[159] Qur'ān 18:46 (Rodwell translation).

[160] Qur'ān 14:24 – 25 (Rodwell translation).

[161] Qur'ān 20:113 (Rodwell translation).

[162] Qur'ān 23:85 (Rodwell translation).

[163] Qur'ān 45:13 (Rodwell translation).

[164] Qur'ān 2:266 (Rodwell translation).

[165] Marcus Aurelius Antoninus Augustus (author), George Long (translator) (1890) *The thoughts of the Emperor Marcus Aurelius Antoninus*, Book VII.

166 Paul Carus (author), Olga Kopetzky (illustrator) (1915) *The Gospel of Buddha, Compiled from Ancient Records*, XCIV, p. 236.

167 Paul Carus (author), Olga Kopetzky (illustrator) (1915) *The Gospel of Buddha, Compiled from Ancient Records*, LIV, p. 163.

168 Paul Carus (author), Olga Kopetzky (illustrator) (1915) *The Gospel of Buddha, Compiled from Ancient Records*, LIV, XXV, pp. 78 – 79.

169 Paul Carus (author), Olga Kopetzky (illustrator) (1915) *The Gospel of Buddha, Compiled from Ancient Records*, LIV, XXV, p. 80.

170 Henry Clarke Warren (1896) *Buddhism in Translations*, § 60. The Forty Subjects of Meditation. Translated from the Visuddhi-Magga (chap. iii.)

171 See: Warren (1896), § 78. The Trance of Cessation. Translated from the Samyutta-Nikâya (xli.6).

172 Plato (author), Benjamin Jowett (translator) (1888) *The Republic of Plato*, Part II, 58, 1.

173 F. Hadland Davis (1920) *Jalálu'd-Dín Rúmí*, p. 88.

174 Thomas à Kempis (author), William Benham (translator) (1886) *The Imitation of Christ* (London: J.C. Nimmo), Chapter XXII. On Meditation upon Death, 3. Available online at: http://www.sacred-texts.com/chr/ioc/index.htm (accessed 25/12/2016).

175 Thomas à Kempis, *The Imitation of Christ*, Ch. XXII, 9.

[176] Marcus Aurelius Antoninus Augustus (author), George Long (translator) (1890) *The thoughts of the Emperor Marcus Aurelius Antoninus*, Book IX.

[177] Thomas à Kempis, *The Imitation of Christ*, Ch. XX, 1, 5 - 6.

[178] Job 33:4 (King James Bible).

[179] Kaiten Nukariya (1913) *The Religion of the Samurai, A Study of Zen Philosophy and Discipline in China and Japan* (Auckland: Floating Press), Ch. VIII. Available online at: http://www.sacred-texts.com/bud/rosa/index.htm (accessed 26/12/2016).

[180] Kaiten Nukariya (1913) *The Religion of the Samurai, A Study of Zen Philosophy and Discipline in China and Japan*, Ch. VIII.

[181] Kaiten Nukariya (1913) *The Religion of the Samurai, A Study of Zen Philosophy and Discipline in China and Japan*, Ch. VIII.

[182] Nakariya (1913), Ch. VIII.

[183] Paul Carus (author), Olga Kopetzky (illustrator) (1915) *The Gospel of Buddha, Compiled from Ancient Records*, LX – Amitabha, pp. 174 – 175.

[184] Nukariya (1913), Ch. VIII.

[185] See: Ven Pannyavaro (1996-2016) BuddhaNet Basic Buddhism Guide: Loving-Kindness Meditation. *Buddha Dharma Education Association & BuddhaNet*. Available online at:

http://www.buddhanet.net/e-learning/loving-kindness.htm
(accessed 27/12/2016).

[186] Loving-kindness meditation. *The Buddhist Centre: Buddhism for Today.* Available online at: https://thebuddhistcentre.com/text/loving-kindness-meditation (accessed 27/12/2016).

[187] Pannyavaro (1996-2016).

[188] Pannyavaro (1996-2016).

[189] See: Loving-kindness meditation. *The Buddhist Centre: Buddhism for Today.*

[190] See: Loving-kindness meditation. *The Buddhist Centre: Buddhism for Today.*

[191] Paul Carus (author), Olga Kopetzky (illustrator) (1915) *The Gospel of Buddha, Compiled from Ancient Records*, LX – Amitabha, pp. 173 – 174.

[192] See: Barbara O'Brien (2016) The Five Dhyani Buddhas: Amitabha Buddha, Buddha of Boundless Light. *AboutReligion.com.* Available online at: http://buddhism.about.com/od/thetriyaka/ig/Five-Dhyani-Buddhas/Amitabha-Buddha.htm (accessed 30/12/2016).

[193] See: The Editors of Encyclopædia Britannica (2010) Amitabha: Buddhism. *Encyclopædia Britannica.* Available online at: https://www.britannica.com/topic/Amitabha-Buddhism (accessed 30/12/2016).

[194] Yejitsu Okusa (1915) *Principal Teachings of The True Sect of Pure Land* (Kyōto: The Ōtaniha Hongwanji), Chapter IV.

Salvation, pp. 70 – 71. Available online at: http://www.sacred-texts.com/bud/ptpl/index.htm (accessed 30/12/2016).

[195] Okusa (1915), pp. 71 – 72.

[196] Okusa (1915), p. 72.

[197] John 14:6 (King James Bible).

[198] Amitābha (*Wikipedia* article). Available online at: https://en.wikipedia.org/wiki/Amitābha (accessed 30/12/2016 17:39).

[199] Nianfo (*Wikipedia* article). Available online at: https://en.wikipedia.org/wiki/Nianfo (accessed 30/12/2016 17:41).

[200] Nianfo (*Wikipedia* article).

[201] Okusa (1915), p. 77.

[202] Veda-Vyāsa (author), Kisari Mohan Gangulia (translator) (1919) *The Mahabharata of Krishna-Dwaipayana Vyasa*, Book 12 (Part one of three): Santi Parva. Translated into English Prose from the Original Sanskrit Text (Calcutta: D. Bose & Co.), Part 3, Section CCCXLIII, p. 165. Available online at: http://www.sacred-texts.com/hin/m12/index.htm (accessed 30/12/2016).

[203] In the Mahabharata, he says: "My complexion also is of that foremost of gems called Harit. It is for these reasons that I am called by the name of Hari." Veda-Vyāsa (author), Kisari Mohan Gangulia (translator) (1919), Part 3, Section CCCXLIII, p. 160.

204 Hare Krishna (mantra) (*Wikipedia* article). Available online at: https://en.wikipedia.org/wiki/Hare_Krishna_(mantra) (accessed 30/12/2016 18:06).

205 See: Meditation (*ISKCON.org* website). Available online at: http://www.iskcon.org/meditation/ (accessed 30/12/2016).

206 Qur'ān 17:110 (Rodwell translation).

207 Jalālu'd-Dīn Rūmī (author), E.H. Whinfield (translator) (1898) *The Spiritual Couplets of Maulana Jalalu'd-Din Muhammad Rumi* (London: Kegan Paul), Book IV, Story I. Available online at: http://www.sacred-texts.com/isl/masnavi/index.htm (accessed 30/12/2016).

208 Qur'ān 38:29 (Rodwell translation).

209 Thomas à Kempis, *The Imitation of Christ*, Ch. V.

210 Thomas à Kempis, *The Imitation of Christ*, Ch. V.

211 Matthew 13:13 (King James Bible).

212 Qur'ān 65:2 – 3 (Rodwell translation).

213 Qur'ān 24:35 (Rodwell translation).

214 Matthew 5:3 – 12 (King James Bible).

215 Matthew 5:13 – 16 (King James Bible).

216 Qur'ān 18:109 (Rodwell translation).

217 Thomas à Kempis, *The Imitation of Christ*, Ch. XXXIV, 1.

218 Thomas à Kempis, *The Imitation of Christ*, Ch. III, 2.

219 Qur'ān 23:84 – 90 (Rodwell translation).

[220] William Penn's Advice to His Children, at *The Quaker Writings Home Page*. Available online at: http://www.qhpress.org/quakerpages/qwhp/qwhp.htm (accessed 31/12/2016).

[221] Veda-Vyāsa (author), Sir Edwin Arnold (translator) (1900) *The Song Celestial; Or, Bhagavad-Gîtâ (from the Mahâbhârata): Being a Discourse Between Arjuna, Prince of India, and the Supreme Being, Under the Form of Krishna,* Chapter VII.

[222] Krishna, *The Bhagavad-Gita*, Ch. XIII.

[223] Veda-Vyāsa (author), Sir Edwin Arnold (translator) (1900) *The Song Celestial; Or, Bhagavad-Gîtâ (from the Mahâbhârata): Being a Discourse Between Arjuna, Prince of India, and the Supreme Being, Under the Form of Krishna,* Chapter IV.

[224] Confucius (author), James Legge (translator) (1861) *The Chinese Classics — Volume 1: Confucian Analects*, Book VI, Chapter XVIII.

[225] Qur'ān 39:9 (Rodwell translation).

[226] Krishna, *The Bhagavad-Gita*, Chapter VI.

[227] Qur'ān 2:285 (Rodwell translation).

[228] Qur'ān 3:66 (Rodwell translation).

[229] F. Hadland Davis (1920) *Jalálu'd-Dín Rúmí*.

[230] George Fox (author), Rufus M. Jones (editor) (1906) *George Fox: An Autobiography*, Chapter IX.

[231] George Fox, *An Autobiography*, Chapter I.

[232] George Fox, *An Autobiography*, Chapter I.

[233] Abū Hāmid Muhammad ibn Muhammad Al-Ghazālī (author), Claud Field (translator) *The Alchemy of Happiness by Al Ghazzali, Translated from the Hindustani*, Chapter VIII.

[234] 1 John 4:8 (King James Bible).

[235] 1 John 4:16 (King James Bible).

[236] Krishna, *The Bhagavad-Gita*, Chapter XVIII.

[237] George Fox, *An Autobiography*, Chapter I.

[238] Al-Ghazālī, *The Alchemy of Happiness by Al Ghazzali*, Chapter VIII.

[239] Khwāja Shamsu'd-Dīn Muhammad (Hafez of Shiraz) (author), Gertrude Lowthian Bell (translator) (1897) *Poems from the Divan of Hafiz*, XXXVI.

[240] Quoted by St. Thomas Aquinas, in St. Thomas Aquinas (author), The Very Rev. Hugh Pope (translator) (1914) *On Prayer and the Contemplative Life*, Question LXXXI, V., pp. 88 – 89.

[241] Abū Hāmid Muhammad ibn Muhammad Al-Ghazālī (author), Claud Field (translator) *The Alchemy of Happiness by Al Ghazzali, Translated from the Hindustani*, Chapter II.

[242] Zhuangzi (author), Herbert Allen Giles (translator) (1889) *Chuang Tzu, Mystic, Moralist, and Social Reformer* (London: B. Quaritch), Chapter IV, pp. 43 – 45. Available online

at: https://archive.org/details/chuangtzumysticmoochua (accessed 31/12/2016).

243 Zhuangzi, *Chuang Tzu, Mystic, Moralist, and Social Reformer*, Chapter IV, pp. 38 – 45.

244 St. Thomas Aquinas (author), The Very Rev. Hugh Pope (translator) (1914) *On Prayer and the Contemplative Life*, I. Question LXXXIII., p. 75.

245 Zhuangzi, *Chuang Tzu, Mystic, Moralist, and Social Reformer*, Chapter IV, p. 47.

246 Zhuangzi, *Chuang Tzu, Mystic, Moralist, and Social Reformer*, Chapter VI, p. 68.

247 Zhuangzi, *Chuang Tzu, Mystic, Moralist, and Social Reformer*, Chapter VI, pp. 73 – 74.

248 Thomas a Kempis (author), William Benham (translator) (1886) *The Imitation of Christ*, Chapter III, 2.

249 Zhuangzi, *Chuang Tzu, Mystic, Moralist, and Social Reformer*, Chapter V, p. 58.

250 Qur'ān 4:174 (Rodwell translation).

251 Matthew 14:6 – 7 (King James Bible).

252 John 10:9 (King James Bible).

253 Zhuangzi, *Chuang Tzu, Mystic, Moralist, and Social Reformer*, Chapter V, p. 58.

254 Zhuangzi, *Chuang Tzu, Mystic, Moralist, and Social Reformer*, Chapter V, p. 66.

255 St. Thomas Aquinas (author), The Very Rev. Hugh Pope (translator) (1914) *On Prayer and the Contemplative Life*, I. Question LXXXII., p. 51.

256 Al-Ghazālī, *The Alchemy of Happiness by Al Ghazzali*, Chapter VIII.

257 Abū Hāmid Muhammad ibn Muhammad Al-Ghazālī (author), Claud Field (translator) *The Alchemy of Happiness by Al Ghazzali, Translated from the Hindustani*, Introduction.

258 Rev. Heng Sure (2001-2015) On Fasting from a Buddhist's Perspective. *UrbanDharma.org*. Available online at: https://www.urbandharma.org/udharma9/fasting.html (accessed 31/12/2016).

259 Quoted by Zhuangzi, *Chuang Tzu, Mystic, Moralist, and Social Reformer*, Chapter XXIII, p. 303.

260 Fasting in Hinduism. *Hinduism Facts*. Available online at: http://hinduismfacts.org/fasting-in-hinduism/ (accessed 31/12/2016).

261 Same as above.

262 Bhaktivedanta Book Trust International (2002-2015) Why is fasting important? *Krishna.com*. Available online at: http://www.krishna.com/why-fasting-important (accessed 31/12/2016).

263 Veda-Vyāsa (author), Sir Edwin Arnold (translator) (1900) *The Song Celestial; Or, Bhagavad-Gîtâ (from the Mahâbhârata): Being a Discourse Between Arjuna, Prince of*

India, and the Supreme Being, Under the Form of Krishna,
Chapter VI.

²⁶⁴ Krishna, *The Bhagavad-Gita*, Chapter VI.

²⁶⁵ Al-Ghazālī, *The Alchemy of Happiness*, Chapter II.

²⁶⁶ Ghiyāthu'd-Dīn Abu'l-Fath 'Umar ibn Ibrāhīm Nīshāpūrī (Omar Khayyām) (author), Edward Fitzgerald (translator) (1881) *Rubaíyát of Omar Khayyam: the astronomer-poet of Persia*, XXXII.

²⁶⁷ F. Hadland Davis (1920) *Jalálu'd-Dín Rúmí*.

²⁶⁸ Qur'ān 72:75 – 76 (Rodwell translation).

²⁶⁹ Krishna, *The Bhagavad-Gita*, Chapter XII.

²⁷⁰ Paul Carus (author), Olga Kopetzky (illustrator) (1915) *The Gospel of Buddha, Compiled from Ancient Records*, XXVI., pp. 81 – 82.

²⁷¹ F. Hadland Davis (1920) *Jalálu'd-Dín Rúmí*.

²⁷² Qur'ān 17:110 (Rodwell translation).

²⁷³ See: 900+ Names and Titles of God. *Christian Answers Network*. Available online at: http://www.christiananswers.net/dictionary/namesofgod.html (accessed 31/12/2016).

²⁷⁴ Zhuangzi, *Chuang Tzu, Mystic, Moralist, and Social Reformer*, Chapter VI, p. 76.

²⁷⁵ Qur'ān 57:25 (Rodwell translation).

²⁷⁶ Martin Lings (1983) *Muhammad: His Life Based on the Earliest Sources* (New York: Inner Traditions International).

[277] Karen Armstrong (1992) *Muhammad: A Biography of the Prophet* (San Francisco, Calif.: Harper San Fransisco).

[278] F. Hadland Davis (1920) *Jalálu'd-Dín Rúmí.*

[279] Zhuangzi, *Chuang Tzu, Mystic, Moralist, and Social Reformer*, Chapter XIII, pp. 157 – 158.

[280] George Fox (author), Rufus M. Jones (editor) (1906) *George Fox: An Autobiography*, Chapter II.

www.ingramcontent.com/pod-product-compliance
Lightning Source LLC
LaVergne TN
LVHW051041080426
835508LV00019B/1633